NEVER TO RETURN

*Surviving the Worst Combat Loss
in the History of the US Coast Guard*

RANDALL PEFFER AND
COL. ROBERT NERSASIAN

Guilford, Connecticut

An imprint of Globe Pequot

Distributed by NATIONAL BOOK NETWORK

British Library Cataloguing in Publication Information available

Library of Congress Cataloging-in-Publication Data available

ISBN 978-1-4930-3122-1 (paperback)
ISBN 978-1-4930-3123-8 (e-book)

♾™ The paper used in this publication meets the minimum requirements of American National Standard for Information Sciences—Permanence of Paper for Printed Library Materials, ANSI/ NISO Z39.48-1992.

Printed in the United States of America

Contents

PART THREE: THINGS FALL APART

PART FOUR: THE DARKEST HOURS

Authors' Note

THE EVENTS, THE ACTIONS OF INDIVIDUAL MEN, AND THE DIALOGUE IN this book have been carefully reconstructed from our firsthand observations as well as the stories of the men involved, their families, and eyewitnesses. When necessary and appropriate, we have also relied on an extensive collection of relevant books, websites, military records, and the established protocols of operation and communication onboard vessels of the type and vintage of U-255, USS *Leopold*, and USS *Joyce*. As with almost all events with multiple witnesses, sometimes the stories about what happened diverge. When such discrepancies arose during our research, we have gone with the story for which there exists the most corroborating firsthand testimony and evidence.

The genesis for this project lies wholly in the hearts of Tory Nersasian and her father Col. Robert Nersasian, the brother of Nelson "Sparky" Nersasian, one of the twenty-eight survivors of the USS *Leopold* catastrophe. Robert Nersasian completed all of the initial research for this book, including the taping of more than a dozen interviews with veterans and the gathering of reams of declassified material from Navy and Coast Guard archives. Writer Randall Peffer joined this project to collaborate with the Nersasians in undertaking additional research as well as in giving shape to the story. The voice in the wartime narrative is his.

Admiral Neptun presenting Sparky Nersasian with his Purple Heart (posthumously), with sister Anne, niece Alexsandra, nephew Jeremy, and author Robert Nersasian, May 21, 2011. COURTESY ROBERT NERSASIAN.

PREFACE

The Coast Guard at War

WITHIN A FEW HOURS OF ENGLAND DECLARING WAR ON GERMANY IN early September 1939, the Battle of the Atlantic began with a German U-boat attacking and sinking a passenger ship en route from Liverpool, England, to Montreal, Quebec. One week later Canada declared war against Germany. The United States declared neutrality in 1939 and used US Coast Guard cutters in an effort to enforce US neutrality for US merchant vessels transiting between North American ports. Italy sided with Germany in 1940 and committed submarine resources to the Battle of the Atlantic, which would become the longest continuous battle of World War II, running from September 1939 until April 1945 when Germany surrendered to the Allied Forces.

Following Germany's conquest of France in 1940, the burden of battling Germany fell upon England. To be successful, England needed nearly continuous resupply of food provisions, fuel, and warfighting materials from North America and elsewhere to battle the well-supplied German military forces. The great demand had to be met by merchant vessels transiting from North American ports to England's ports across the vast and often volatile North Atlantic Ocean.

An important lesson learned during World War I was that the most successful strategy for resupply of food, fuel, and warfighting materials across the high seas included clustering a flotilla of thirty or more merchant vessels into a convoy escorted by a group of well-armed, agile warships equipped for anti-submarine warfare. England increased merchant vessel shipbuilding in the 1930s, and the Royal Navy prepared for the likelihood of hostilities during that period by building new classes of frigates and corvettes equipped with the latest anti-submarine warfare technology. During the 1930s the US Coast Guard constructed the Secretary Class of high-endurance cutters, which were well suited for convoy escort duties. These 327-foot cutters would become part of the initial US convoy escort response against German U-boats.

The origin of the US Coast Guard dates back to the earliest years of America's democracy when the first secretary of the treasury, Alexander Hamilton, persuaded Congress to authorize and fund construction of ten small cutters, with experienced crews, to patrol US coastal waters, forming the nucleus of the new US Revenue Marine. Their primary mission was to reduce smuggling of imported goods and ensure all merchant vessels paid import duties to help build the US Treasury and reduce the national debt accumulated during the Revolutionary War.

Freedom to transit across the high seas and to conduct coastwise trading was critical to US national interests and survival of the nation. It did not take long for the early cutters of the Revenue Marine to be dispatched farther offshore to provide safe passage for US merchant vessels that were occasionally boarded on the high seas and seized by warships from England or France. These so-called "revenue cutters" also battled opportunistic pirate vessels along the southeast Atlantic coast and in the Gulf of Mexico and Caribbean Sea to reclaim seized cargoes and to free American crewmembers taken hostage and forced to work aboard their captors' ships.

In the late 1790s, the president and Congress could see that naval hostilities were inevitable with France, and they began rebuilding the Continental Navy that had been decommissioned at the end of the Revolutionary War. As naval vessels were commissioned, Navy crews and Revenue Marine crews protected US shipping interests and fought back French efforts to control the sea lanes on the high seas. This Quasi-War with France was the first use of revenue cutters and US Navy ships to fight together against foreign aggressors.

Just over a decade later, the United States found itself at war with England in the War of 1812. Revenue cutters complemented the capabilities of the US Navy, and the die was cast for moving the US Revenue Marine into the Navy Department during wartime. Later in the nineteenth century, the Revenue Marine was renamed the US Revenue Cutter

Service. During this period, the Revenue Cutter Service demonstrated its leadership and abilities by providing safe passage along the coastal sea lanes and on the high seas. Congress rewarded the service with additional responsibilities that ranged from winter North Atlantic safety patrols to African slave trade patrols. Revenue cutters also served in the Seminole Indian Wars (1836–1842), the Mexican War (1846–1848), the Civil War (1861–1865), and the Spanish-American War (1898).

The modern US Coast Guard was formed by bringing two government agencies (the US Lifesaving Service and the US Revenue Cutter Service) together in 1915. US involvement in the war being fought in Europe seemed inevitable, and this consolidation of maritime agencies would be helpful if war was declared. In April 1917, German U-boats destroyed five US merchant vessels, which led President Wilson to ask Congress to declare war against Germany. Within several days, the president moved the US Coast Guard under the operational control of the secretary of the navy.

The US war effort quickly accelerated, and within a few months, six Coast Guard cutters were dispatched to the Navy's Atlantic Fleet, serving as convoy escorts between Gibraltar and the British Isles. The six cutters (*Algonquin*, *Manning*, *Ossipee*, *Seneca*, *Tampa*, and *Yamacraw*) proved to be agile escorts, well suited for confronting German U-boats as they prepared to attack US and British convoys. Tragically, USCGC *Tampa* was sunk in the Celtic Sea by a German U-boat on the evening of September 26, 1918, after successfully escorting her eighteenth convoy. All of *Tampa*'s 115 crewmembers were lost at sea, the largest loss of life for a US naval vessel during World War I.

In the spring of 1941, President Roosevelt declared Iceland and Greenland to be protectorates of the United States, and the Coast Guard was tasked with patrolling their coastal waters in search of German vessels or others attempting to establish bases near the vital sea lanes between Greenland and Iceland. By the summer of 1941, the United States was still months away from formally entering World War II. President Roosevelt and Prime Minister Churchill met in Newfoundland to discuss supply line threats and movement of food, material, and warfighting equipment from North America to England. They both agreed that Allied control of the sea lanes in the North Atlantic was critical in their effort to curtail the Axis threat to the food, fuel, and war materials "pipeline" established along the North Atlantic sea routes. On November 1, the US Coast Guard was transferred to the Navy Department to serve in whatever tasks were necessary to better prepare the sea services for war. Pearl Harbor was attacked on December 7, and Hitler declared war on the United States on December 11.

Following the Pearl Harbor attack, tens of thousands of young Americans joined the US military. In the ten weeks following Pearl Harbor, just over ten thousand Americans enlisted in the active duty Coast Guard and reserve. By summer 1942, the US Coast Guard had grown to over sixty thousand military personnel, with the service reaching its peak in June 1944 at just over 177,700 personnel on active duty and in the reserve. During World War II, a total of 214,239 personnel served on US Coast Guard active duty or in the Coast Guard Reserve.* The service grew tenfold between 1941 and 1944 to respond to the wartime demands of the multi-mission Coast Guard. Coast Guardsmen served in convoy escort divisions; on troop transport ships, amphibious ships, beach landing craft, and coastal picket vessels; and performed duties including port security, hazardous materials loading, and beach and harbor patrol.

US shipbuilding capacity was accelerated at record pace as soon as the United States entered World War II. Some of the Lend-Lease shipbuilding for England was diverted to provide convoy escort ships for US Navy and US Coast Guard crews. But ships were being redesigned and reconfigured to meet the needs of US and Allied sea services. Destroyer escorts, ships from 283 feet to 306 feet in length, with the latest anti-submarine warfare equipment, were constructed and launched from a variety of shipyards in America's ports. Eighty-five of the 306-foot *Edsall* Class destroyer escorts were built during World War II. Thirty of the *Edsall* Class escorts were manned by Coast Guard crews, serving with distinction in the North Atlantic and elsewhere. These ships were well suited for convoy escort duties and anti-submarine warfare.

Among these new destroyer escorts was USS *Leopold* (DE 319), launched on June 12, 1943. Her loss on March 9, 1944, with 171 of her

---

*Coast Guard History, www.uscg.mil/history/faqs/WWIIpersonnel.asp.

crewmembers—following a battle with U-255 south of Iceland—represents the second largest loss of life aboard a US Coast Guard ship in the history of a proud service, the single largest loss of life in the combat history of the US Coast Guard, and the first destroyer escort lost in World War II. The survival and resilience of twenty-eight of her men in the icy North Atlantic stand as an inspiration and a lesson in survival to Coast Guard crews, all mariners, and anyone faced with sudden and unimaginable catastrophe.

Colonel Nersasian and Randall Peffer thoroughly researched the history of USS *Leopold* along with the personal stories from her Coast Guard crewmembers and their families. With their book *Never to Return*, the authors have added great depth to the historical narrative of US Coast Guard–manned destroyer escorts in the Battle of the Atlantic and spotlighted the stories of honor, respect, and devotion to duty of these Coast Guardsmen during World War II.

—D. A. Neptun, RADM, USCG (Retired)

INTRODUCTION

NELSON "SPARKY" NERSASIAN, MY OLDER BROTHER AND MENTOR, DIED in 1997. He was twenty-one years old when I was born and was soon to serve in the US Coast Guard in the seas of the North Atlantic. His World War II service was reflected in the *Semper Paratus* tattoo on his right upper arm. Those Latin words are the US Coast Guard's motto. They mean "Always Ready." It would be many years before I fully understood the significance of those words and my brother's tattoo.

Decades passed before I grasped what Sparky had endured on March 9, 1944, south of Iceland. He was among twenty-eight men to survive the German torpedo attack on his destroyer escort (DE) USS *Leopold* while on convoy duty. Manned by a Coast Guard crew, it was the first destroyer escort lost in World War II. The ship broke in half and sunk. One hundred and seventy-one of Sparky's shipmates perished in the icy waters. Their deaths mark the worst wartime disaster in US Coast Guard history.

Dr. Tory Nersasian.
COURTESY ROBERT NERSASIAN.

In 1986 my daughter, Tory Nersasian, was assigned a project to interview someone who had been to war by her honors history teacher Donald Doliber at Masconomet Regional High School in Topsfield, Massachusetts. The assignment was an exercise in interview techniques as well as a history lesson about a family member or friend who had served in a war. Like me, Tory knew that her Uncle Sparky had served in World War II, but was unaware of the extent of his experiences.

Unable to find a better tape recorder, she grabbed her younger brother's Fisher-Price toy recorder, inserted a used, inexpensive cassette tape, and began to ask Sparky questions about his Coast Guard experience in the war. For the next twenty-three years, that cassette tape remained packed and forgotten until rediscovered after Tory's move to central California.

As readers will see in the prologue to this volume, listening to that old tape changed my daughter. Her heart flooded with feelings, and her mind began seething with questions. She started searching the Internet for information about the *Leopold* disaster. She found short articles concerning the *Leopold* but no real factual details of the ship's history and demise. Seeing old interviews with survivors posted on YouTube deepened her curiosity. She learned that the *Leopold* was on her second voyage,

Tape used in Fisher-Price toy recorder for Sparky interview.
COURTESY ROBERT NERSASIAN.

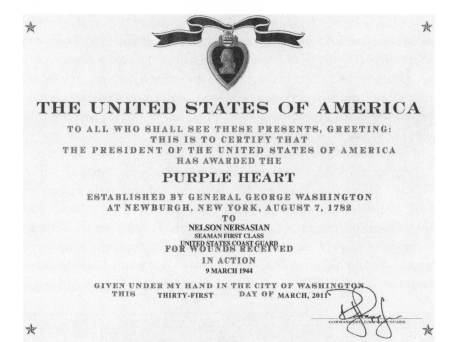

THE UNITED STATES OF AMERICA

TO ALL WHO SHALL SEE THESE PRESENTS, GREETING:
THIS IS TO CERTIFY THAT
THE PRESIDENT OF THE UNITED STATES OF AMERICA
HAS AWARDED THE

PURPLE HEART

ESTABLISHED BY GENERAL GEORGE WASHINGTON
AT NEWBURGH, NEW YORK, AUGUST 7, 1782
TO

NELSON NERSASIAN
SEAMAN FIRST CLASS
UNITED STATES COAST GUARD

FOR WOUNDS RECEIVED
IN ACTION
9 MARCH 1944

GIVEN UNDER MY HAND IN THE CITY OF WASHINGTON
THIS   THIRTY-FIRST   DAY OF MARCH, 2011

COMMANDANT, USCG COAST GUARD

Sparky Nersasian's Purple Heart. COURTESY ROBERT NERSASIAN.

almost completely manned by inexperienced teenagers, and led by young officers in their early twenties.

Further digging revealed that just prior to engaging the German submarine U-255, the convoy commander had switched the *Leopold*'s position with another destroyer escort. Why had the vessel with the less-experienced crew and leadership ended up as the one to directly investigate the U-boat radar contact and engage the enemy? Why did none of the officers survive the sinking? How in the cold air and water and high seas did twenty-eight seamen last through the night? Why was the USS *Joyce* delayed for more than two hours in its attempts to rescue all those men from the *Leopold* who had abandoned ship?

Each tidbit of information spawned more questions and urged Tory to dig deeper. Through contacts established online, she discovered that seaman Harry Daube, assumed to be the last living survivor of the *Leopold*, had been awarded the Purple Heart on June 4, 2010. Wondering why her Uncle Sparky had never received a Purple Heart for the shrapnel wounds and hypothermia he endured, she knew there was still work to be done. Inquiries with the US Coast Guard led her to the Office of Awards and Ceremonies of the Coast Guard in Washington, DC. After a thorough review of the records, the Coast Guard determined that Sparky was indeed eligible for the award.

COAST GUARD Compass

Official Blog of the U.S. Coast Guard

WWII Coast Guardsman receives Purple Heart

Sunday, June 6, 2010

Posted by: Christopher Lagan

Senior Chief Petty Officer Michael Jensen pins a Purple Heart onto the chest of WWII Coast Guardsman Harry Milton Daube. (U.S. Coast Guard photo by Petty Officer 3rd Class Cindy Beckert)

USS Leopold at her launching in 1943. (U.S. Naval Historical Center Photograph)

http://coastguard.dodlive.mil/2010/06/wwii-coast-guardsman-receives-purple-heart/   11/16/2011

Purple Heart for *Leopold* Coast Guardsman Harry Milton Daube, June 4, 2010. COURTESY USCG.

In 2011 our family and friends gathered at Winter Island Park in Salem, Massachusetts, for a Coast Guard ceremony to award Sparky the Purple Heart he had earned so long ago in the cold, dark seas south of Iceland. This could have ended the story. Sparky had his award. Our family could have walked away and gotten on with our lives. But what about the lives of all those others who perished on that moonlit night in 1944? What about the twenty-eight who survived? Were others still alive? If so, they had stories and nightmares that needed answers.

Where were their awards? Who would provide answers for their families? Did they not deserve the same recognition that had just been given Sparky? What about the men of the USS *Joyce* who plucked survivors out of the freezing Atlantic?

I knew the answer. Sparky was not just my big brother. He was my best friend, my mentor, my coach, and my best man. At twenty-one years old he was thrust into a world war. Inexperienced and naïve, he had seen friends terribly wounded in combat on the open seas. He had seen friends drown. He had seen them die of exposure, seen a few just swim off never to be seen again. It was a quantum test of survival, a test he endured every day for the rest of his life.

The records were wrong. There were more living survivors. There were more stories to be told, truths to be unearthed. This book is an attempt to tell those stories of tragedy, miraculous survival, and heroism to honor all those men who died and those few who survived. This narrative also offers the possibility of closure for those who survived and for all the families of missing veterans who have spent countless moments wondering when, how, and why.

—Col. Robert Nersasian

Prologue

"We were heading northeast toward Ireland in an area they called 'Torpedo Junction.' They called it that because that's where the U-boats sat and waited for the convoys like us," says the voice rising from the stereo speakers. The voice is grandfatherly, warm and resonant with a clipped Boston accent. "It's 7:30 at night and freezing cold, colder than the shades of hell. Take your candy bar and place it outside and it froze solid in ten minutes."

Forward deck 3"/50 gun on the USS *Slater* (same as gun Sparky manned on the *Leopold*). COURTESY *USS SLATER*, DESTROYER ESCORT HISTORICAL MUSEUM, ALBANY, NEW YORK.

Tory Nersasian feels her stomach tighten, realizes that she has been holding her breath. The voice she is listening to is her Uncle Sparky's. He has been dead for thirteen years, but he's talking to her as she sits on the couch in the living room of her new home in Atascadero, California. The afternoon sun is pouring in through the picture window and bathing the green, tree-covered hills in the distance. But sitting here on the living room couch, she's feeling frozen as her uncle's voice begins to recount his escape from a nightmare.

As a teenager she interviewed her uncle for a history class project about his experience on convoy duty as a Coast Guard seaman aboard the destroyer escort USS *Leopold*. Now twenty-four years later she has rediscovered the tape of the interview among a box of cassettes by U2, Fleetwood Mac, and Def Leppard left over from her teens. For almost two decades she has been lugging this box of tapes with her across the country from her childhood home in coastal Massachusetts. And today, after this latest move to California, she has decided finally to face off with these tapes and discard a whole lot of memories from her girlhood.

Sparky in the 1950s, back in the grocery business. COURTESY ROBERT NERSASIAN.

Up to this point the discarding has been easy because tape after tape has broken when put in the stereo's tape player. But, this one, the one simply labeled "Uncle Sparky's story," is coming through loud and clear, against all odds. It's as if Sparky's calling to her, she thinks, reaching out.

"We're seven hundred miles from Ireland," he says. "General Quarters sounds and we're in the ready gun with a skeleton crew. Waves are rolling over the deck, a wall of water."

She shivers. Scenes from the movie *Titanic* are starting to scroll through her mind. She can picture her uncle among the *Titanic's* crew struggling to save the ship and all those people going into the North Atlantic after the liner rams the iceberg. She can see that wiry body in the blue uniform with his cocked grin beneath his white sailor's cap. Sparky to the rescue.

Growing up, she loved Sparky Nersasian as if he were her grandfather. He never married. After his Coast Guard service in World War II, he had moved back home with his parents in Salem, Massachusetts, and never left. He cared for them in their old age and mentored his niece through her youth with his optimism, his delight in ironies, his ready

Sparky and father postwar in family grocery store. COURTESY ROBERT NERSASIAN.

laughter, and his gentleness. He was the relative who took over the family's mom-and-pop convenience store, the man who always made sure to sneak his niece chocolate Easter bunnies when her parents weren't looking, the magician who taught her card tricks, the MENSA member, the teller of fabulous tales. He was the spirit who came to her and gave her peace a few years ago when she was riding in a light plane. Its engine failed, and the plane crash-landed just a mile short of the Grand Canyon. It was as if Sparky were sitting next to her on that plane, telling her everything was going to be all right.

Now he seems to be asking for some help, saying, "Listen to me. Nobody knows the horror that I escaped."

The tape rolls on. "I'm the pointer, the one that makes it [the gun] go up and down. On my right is Jerry Claus, the trainer. He makes it go left and right. Behind me is a guy called the captain, Gun Captain Bradley, and behind him is a guy called Zombie who takes care of the shells. . . ."

As a teenager hearing this story, Nersasian had been entertained by the vividness of the narrative, the crispness of her uncle's memory. Her uncle's laughter put her at ease at moments when he talked about a guy they called Zombie. But now at age forty, she hears something different. Sparky's story sounds epic, horrifying, sinister.

"We look up and there is a sub in front of us . . . everybody's yelling, 'Get those bastards. Kill them. Kill them.' The sub is going across us right to left on top of the water . . . someone says, 'Torpedo,' and there we are wide open. Absolutely no defense. Bang. Explosion. Thought I would never hear another sound in my life."

Nersasian is a psychologist. She has worked with veterans, and now she's realizing that as her uncle gets deeper into his story, she's hearing the detachment, the emotional dissociation, common in the narratives of warriors suffering from what used to be called "shell shock," PTSD.

"The ship is in two pieces, just held together by the deck. Everything was sliding toward the center of the ship. Cut in half just like you measured it. Down we went."

This is not her office. This is not a clinical interview or a counseling session. This is her uncle speaking to her. "Tory, listen." She's not religious, not sure that she believes in a higher power, but Uncle Sparky has always seemed "magical." That was her preferred word for him when she was a kid. Now he's working his magic again, speaking to her from across time and space, from beyond death.

"Jerry is looking at me, but he doesn't know me. I don't know what happened, whether he got hit with a piece of metal or in the shock of the hit he banged his head on the scope. I put a life jacket on him anyway. It was the last time I saw him . . . the last I saw of him."

As the bow begins to tear away from the rest of the ship, Sparky finds a life vest. He has on four or five layers of clothes, heavy gloves, buckled-on hat, jacket, woolen facemask.

"That's how cold it was and ice was hanging from the end of your nose. It was just terrible."

The tape runs for another forty minutes, laden with excruciating details about men sinking into the black icy water, about overturned and overloaded life rafts, about the DE USS *Joyce* arriving to rescue the *Leopold*'s men in the water, but steaming away because she thinks she is under attack by torpedoes. Hours pass, seas build. Men are screaming for Jesus and their mothers. Their limbs are swelling to twice their normal size. Before the *Joyce* returns, men become floating ice statues; many just fall asleep never to wake.

"This man is in the water. Three or four feet away. You can't help him. He's a dead man. Out of the two hundred guys, less than thirty make it out," says Sparky.

Once again, Nersasian is seeing scenes from *Titanic*, the ones with all those floating, frozen bodies in life vests. She feels the piercing chill of the water pressing in on her body, but hot tears forming in her eyes. And Uncle Sparky's voice is killing her as the tape ends.

"Now that I think about it, I wonder, what was it all about? What's the sense? They killed two hundred [*sic*] of my friends. And my gun was responsible for maybe killing some mother's son, some woman's husband, sweetheart. Just human beings."

She can't help herself. She's crying now, feeling her uncle's unresolved grief about all those men lost on the night of March 9, 1944, feeling his regrets and survivor's guilt, too. She's wondering by what miracle was his life spared that night. And she's wondering about how the fates have dealt with the other men and families of the *Leopold*.

She has to call Massachusetts. She wants to hear her dad's husky, baritone voice, wants to say, "Dad, you won't believe this."

Cast of Characters

USS *Leopold*:
Kenneth C. Phillips, captain, bridge of the ship
Burtis P. Cone, executive officer, bridge of the ship
William N. Tillman, ensign, stern of the ship
Charles W. Valaer, ensign, stern of the ship
Aram "Sparky" Nersasian, number two gun crew, bow of the ship
Lucas L. Bobbitt, number two gun crew, bow of the ship
Charles F. H. Bradley, number two gun captain, bow of the ship
Gerald W. Claus, number two gun crew, bow of the ship
Harry M. Daube, number three gun crew, stern of the ship
Gale L. Fuller, number six K-gun crew, stern of the ship
William J. Miller, captain's talker, bridge of the ship
Joseph Armand Burgun, captain's talker/signalman, bridge of ship
Walter L. Ward, radioman, bridge of ship
Richard Forrester, number seven K-gun crew, stern of the ship
Chester Piechal, stern of the ship
Robert E. Chandler, 40mm clip room, bow of the ship
Jeremiah J. Bowen, third repair party, stern of the ship
Glyone R. Mahaffy, talker on the spotter and setter, stern of the ship
Warren B. Young, 40mm director, stern of the ship
Richard R. Novotny, 20mm gunner, middle of the ship

USS *Joyce*:
Robert Wilcox, captain of the rescue ship
Kingdrel N. Ayres, executive officer
Harry H. Ham Jr., first lieutenant
John L. Bender, ASW officer

Daniel H. Kimball, pharmacist's mate
Barney Olsen, radar operator
Gerald Stern, signalman on flying bridge
Monty Coulter, repair party

U-255:
Erich Harms, captain of the submarine that torpedoed the *Leopold*
Dieter Hengen, first watch officer

PART ONE
SETTING SAIL

Chapter One

Leaving Home

After Pearl Harbor

THEY WERE JUST BOYS, THOSE SAILORS OF USS *LEOPOLD*, USS *JOYCE*, and the other four destroyer escorts of Escort Division 22. That's what Sparky Nersasian and his surviving shipmates will so often say about themselves and their US Coast Guard service decades later when they unfold the nightmare of March 9, 1944. Just boys like most of the other 16.1 million American veterans of World War II, just boys like most of those 407,000 sailors, soldiers, and airmen who did not return home alive from their service. Just boys like nineteen hundred Coast Guard seamen lost in the war. Just ordinary American boys.

But Tory Nersasian will discover that her Uncle Sparky, Nelson Nersasian Jr., and these other sailors of the *Leopold*, *Joyce*, and Escort Division 22's Task Group 21.5 are far from ordinary. Each arrives at that watery battleground south of Iceland on the night of March 9, 1944, with a different story. Each finds his own private path to heroism. And each man's story haunts his family in peculiar ways.

Nelson Nersasian's story starts long before he gained his nickname. He became Sparky in the Coast Guard. But on the morning of December 8, 1941, he is still known to his family and friends by his Armenian name, Aram. It's a little after 6:00 in the morning when he begins to move the early-morning deliveries of fresh milk and newspapers off the sidewalk in front of his father's convenience store Nelson's Spa on the corner of Boston and Essex Streets in Salem, Massachusetts.

Another Monday morning. Another week of work at the Spa. He feels stuck. He and his younger brother Art have been working here at the store after school and on Saturdays for as long as he can remember. His older sister Anne and younger sister Rose work here too. But he's a high school graduate now, out of Salem High School more than two years. At home he spends hours listening to Beethoven symphonies and sonatas on his collection of 78 rpm discs. Recently he has discovered opera, especially the work of Verdi and Puccini. Every time he hears Francesco Merli's recording of the aria "Nessun Dorma" from Puccini's *Turandot*, he wants to spread his arms like wings and fly far from Salem. He has dreams of exploring a world beyond this small coastal city steeped in Puritan history and teeming with Irish, Italian, French, and Polish immigrants.

Armenian families are fiercely loyal, and he feels that he owes it to his parents to help them with the family business. His father deserves a break. The man came to the United States as a refugee of the Armenian Holocaust. Nerses Nersasian, known to the patrons at his Spa as Nelson, has only spoken about the Holocaust once, but his oldest son has never forgotten. The story haunts him, hurts his heart. His father told him that when he was sixteen years old, he hid behind a curtain in a church and watched Turkish horsemen kill his parents. The Turks speared his parents to the altar. He lost eleven of his thirteen siblings to the Turks, but escaped with an older sister by hiding in a haystack and a well.

The sun's not up yet this morning, but the headlights of morning commuters have begun to crawl up the street toward Boston. He shivers as he totes the bundles of newspapers into the shop. With the compact body and strength of an acrobat, he slings the bundles on the floor of the shop in front of the news rack, rubs his hands together to ward off the chills. Wondering if today will bring relief from the cold front that blasted through New England yesterday, he grabs the top copy of the *Boston Daily Globe* and searches the upper left corner of the front page for the weather report. He's reading that it will be "warmer today," when his eyes catch on the headlines.

HAWAII BOMBED
JAPAN DECLARES WAR

He sees pictures of exploded aircraft and sunken, burning ships at Pearl Harbor. But his mind does not fill in the soundtrack of whining planes and exploding bombs. His mind hears something like the fugal battle music of Verdi's *Macbeth*. These soaring melodies are perhaps the strangest call to arms a young man of only twenty-one has ever heard, but the youth who will become Sparky is far from commonplace. This lover of opera, Mozart, and Shakespeare yearns to enter the fray, yearns to defend his country. But how, where, when? He reaches for a fresh pack of Luckies behind the cash register; a smoke might calm his mind.

Crewman Armand Burgun on the USS *Leopold*, 1943. COURTESY BURGIN FAMILY ARCHIVES.

Unlike the hundreds of thousands of volunteers who besiege the recruiting offices of the Army, Navy, and Coast Guard in the weeks following the Japanese attack on Pearl Harbor, Aram Nersasian takes another year to disentangle himself from Nelson's Spa and take the plunge. One of the things that may be holding him back is that his dad, well into his sixties, is fretting about how to manage the store with Aram wanting to leave for the service and his brother Art off in college at MIT. Perhaps he has also figured out from the whispering between his parents that his family is about to have a surprise. His mother is four months pregnant. So his parents are more than a little reluctant with their support when he volunteers for the US Coast Guard on November 9, 1942, at the Coast Guard recruiting office at 70 State Street, Boston. About six weeks later he takes a train from Boston to New York City and reports for boot camp at the US Maritime Service Training Station at Sheepshead Bay, New York, at the east end of Brooklyn, on January 27, 1943.

Although Nersasian does not know it yet, he is in step with most of his shipmates on the USS *Leopold*. J. Armand Burgun arrives at this training facility that the coasties call "Manhattan Beach" in July 1942 at the age of sixteen. Born as the son of a traveling salesman in Rochester, New York, young Burgun has moved with his family at least once every two years. He has lied about his age to a recruiter and slipped into the Coast Guard looking to put a little stability in his life and test his mettle. He will be the youngest man on the *Leopold*'s crew and the last man rescued alive.

Nersasian and Burgun's shipmate Harry Daube, from New York, is twenty and looking for adventure when he arrives at Manhattan Beach with a gang of local recruits. Gale Fuller from Minnetonka, Minnesota, an all-state footballer in high school, lands at boot camp more or less by happenstance. He had enlisted in the Marines, but a friend who was joining the Coast Guard persuaded him to switch. A congenial recruiting officer has helped him to make the swap.

Unlike these other men, Charles Francis Huntington "Fran" Bradley will reach the *Leopold* as a married man. He has a baby girl, Mary Frances, born on Christmas Day, 1942. Bradley was a police officer and Marine reservist in Washington, DC, before the war. But since Pearl Harbor he has been on active duty guarding coastie bases on the Great Lakes. Recently, he has been transferred into the Coast Guard and he worries about being ordered to sea and leaving his wife Dorothy, whom he calls "Toots," home alone in Ashland, Wisconsin. Still, he's an eternal optimist and tells her with his characteristic, light-hearted confidence that everything will turn out all right. She is far from sure.

William J. Miller from Auburn Heights, Michigan, has always dreamed of going to sea. Something about the rootlessness of being a mariner appeals to him. He signs up for the Coast Guard with his two brothers in Cleveland, Ohio, in August 1942. Bill is eighteen but his brothers are younger and lie about their ages. They head off for training at the Coast Guard Station in Erie, Pennsylvania.

Walter Lee Ward comes to the Coast Guard later in life than most of his shipmates. He has been working in a shipyard in Orange, Texas, that is building destroyer escorts. Their sleek, no-nonsense looks inspire him to sign up for sea duty. As he heads off for Basic Training, he has no idea that he will see these ships again, no idea that they will be the last ships he sees before the North Atlantic steals his life. But maybe he senses that he doesn't have all the time in the world, because before he leaves to become a coastie, he marries his wife Ann and fathers a son, Walter Lee Ward Jr.

Some of the enlisted men destined for Escort Division 22—like the *Leopold*'s Miller and Bradley, and the *Joyce*'s Gerald Stern of Chicago and Monty Coulter from Maryland—do their Basic Training elsewhere. But most of the men of Escort Division 22 pass through Manhattan Beach.

Barney Olsen arrives at Manhattan Beach on his way to join the *Joyce* under somewhat false pretenses. He has grown up on Staten Island, but he was born in Norway and his parents never quite got around to getting Barney his citizenship papers. He tried to enlist in the Navy, but was rejected because of his inability to prove his citizenship. It was when he was leaving the Navy enlistment office in Manhattan with a glum look on his face that a Coast Guard recruiter spotted him and offered him immediate enlistment if he promised to bring citizenship papers to the office before being bussed off to Manhattan Beach. He never brought the papers and the Coast Guard never asked.

CHAPTER TWO

Becoming Coasties

1942–1943, Manhattan Beach

"WHAT ARE YOU MADE OF, SEAMAN?" THE DRILL INSTRUCTOR IS BARKing at Aram Nersasian. "Put up those dukes and show us whether you are a man or a mouse."

Nersasian feels his fists tighten inside the impossibly large sixteen-ounce boxing gloves. The protective headgear pinches the sides of his head as he steps toward the middle of the boxing ring to face off with a man who has the cruel smile of a seasoned thug. In fact, the man is a professional boxer . . . and a drill instructor. Each trainee in Nersasian's platoon has to go a round, three minutes, in the ring with this pro or someone like him.

Manhattan Beach is a huge training camp less than a mile from the boardwalk, arcade, and roller coasters of Coney Island. Following the Japanese attack on Pearl Harbor, the Coast Guard bought 125 acres on the eastern end of Brooklyn for the Sheepshead Bay Maritime Service station. When it opens in September 1942, it is a vast blend of beach bungalows that have been turned into barracks, quickly built Quonset huts, mess halls, parade ground, obstacle courses, the landlocked training ship USCGC *Neversail*, dusty roads, port facilities, and, of course, this gym. Sheepshead Bay is a city within a city. It handles ten thousand trainees at a time, and will graduate more than thirty-five thousand in a year. Radio commentator Walter Winchell has called Manhattan Beach the only legal concentration camp in the world. Some of the trainees refer to the camp facetiously as the "Garden of Eden."

During their eight to twelve weeks at Manhattan Beach, these boys from places like Massachusetts, Minnesota, New York, Maryland, Wisconsin, and Texas acquire the basic skills they need to be coasties. They rise at 0530 hours every morning. They learn how to march and salute, how to dress for inspection and keep their personal space shipshape. They launch, row, and retrieve pulling boats from the beach. They go to the firing range to practice with small arms and heavy weapons like the 20mm and 40mm twin or quad mounts, the three-inch 50-caliber, and the five-inch 38-caliber open mount. They spend days firing at an aerial target towed up and down a beach.

They learn how to close watertight doors, pump water from one ship's compartment to another, how to shore up a damaged hull, how to survive a burning ship with oxygen masks, and how to abandon ship without a lifeboat. They strap into life jackets, hold their noses, grab their family jewels, and jump twenty feet into a tank of water with a fire flaring on top. They swim out of the flames, splashing water to keep their hair and eyebrows from catching fire. They practice cold-water survival.

Aboard the *Neversail* they tie knots, make rope fenders, splice rope and wire. They master the names of all the lines and make the *Neversail* ready to go to sea. They practice landing a ship at a dock and tying it up. They set the bow anchors, rig a sea anchor, and fix a scramble net over the side to pick up men in the water. And when their day is done, they gather in the mess halls to feast on a stew known as "frickin' chick-a-sea." Finally, they survive sleepless, booze-soaked liberties in Manhattan.

But for Nersasian and a lot of other trainees, this class in physical defense is the one thing they will remember most about boot camp. These moments in the boxing ring are the ones they write home about. They tell their families that boxing at Manhattan Beach is the experience that gives them the confidence to persevere against all odds. None other than the celebrated heavyweight boxing champion of the world Jack Dempsey is the director of physical education here. He enlisted after Pearl Harbor as a lieutenant. The champ has already risen to the rank of lieutenant commander, and he has hired a cadre of professional boxers to turn these boys to men.

Remember These Important Things From Your Physical Training Course In The Coast Guard Training Station, Manhattan Beach.

1. A good offense is the best defense.

2. Get off first, hit the enemy before he hits you.

3. Keep your hands up at all times.

4. Always keep your chin down.

5. Always keep your left hand out in your opponent's face, don't drop your hands after punching.

6. When you leave here, keep yourself in condition by doing roadwork, shadow boxing, calisthenics and any exercise that will keep you fit. All competitive sports are fine. This may be the saving of your life as well as thousands of others.

7. Have confidence in yourself, remember when you are tired your enemy may be more tired; keep on punching. Remember we have but one aim, and that is to win this war, and by keeping yourself in condition, the job will be finished that much sooner.

You have now completed your course in Physical Fitness and we appreciate your splendid spirit and cooperation while here at Manhattan Beach.

Good Luck To You From

Lieutenant Commander Jack Dempsey and Staff

Jack Dempsey, world heavyweight boxing champion and US Coast Guard instructor at Manhattan Beach during World War II. COURTESY US COAST GUARD TRAINING STATION, MANHATTAN BEACH.

So, now, as Aram Nersasian raises his gloves on guard in front of his chin and eyes the pug-nosed assassin moving toward him, the scrawny Armenian shop-boy from Salem, Massachusetts, tries to muster some pluck. He reaches deep into himself for the fire that he used to chase bullies away from his younger brother Art back on the grade-school playground. He knows that a mouse turns his head away from his enemy and runs. But a man holds eye contact, takes slow, deep breaths, and moves head-on toward an opponent. Nersasian's going to do this the Coast Guard way, or die trying. *Semper Paratus*, Always Ready. The only question is who will throw the first punch.

"Come on, kid. Show me what you got. Show me. . . ."

The thug is spitting his taunts through his mouthpiece when Nersasian feels the heat rising inside him and lets loose with a left jab for the head. But the boxer jerks back with his upper body and takes the blow on his gloves.

For several seconds the fighters back away from each other and circle. Then the kid tucks his chin and attacks.

He jabs with his right then hurls a left, right combination of hooks. His arms feel on fire.

The jab doesn't get by the boxer, but the fast-following hooks glance off the opponent's headgear.

"Whoa," says the instructor, dancing out of range. "Look at Sparky go."

"Hit him," someone shouts from ringside. "Hit him again, Sparky."

But Nersasian's too distracted by this Sparky-business to throw a punch. Next thing he knows he's lying flat on his back. The room is spinning around him. But he gets up, charges his enemy with both arms swinging . . . and a nickname that will stick with him for life.

Chapter Three

Learning the Ropes

1942–1943 at Sea

WHILE SPARKY NERSASIAN, BARNEY OLSEN, AND THEIR FUTURE SHIP-
mates are facing off with boot camp at places like Manhattan Beach, the
man destined to be the commanding officer on the USS *Joyce,* Robert
Wilcox, is coming off watch as an engineering officer in the high latitudes
of the North Atlantic. It's midnight. The cutter is making 30-degree rolls
port and starboard in heavy beam seas. For the last four hours, Wilcox
has been tending to the Babcock & Wilcox boilers in the 240-foot Coast
Guard cutter USS *Modoc.* But now in his tiny cabin he packs his pipe
with Heines Blend tobacco and laces it with a little Amphora for that
rich fragrance of oranges, raspberries, and flowers. Then he lights up.

USS *Joyce.* COURTESY NATIONAL ARCHIVES.

It seems like the only place he has seen for days, weeks maybe, has been this cabin or the steamy engine room of the *Modoc*. What he wouldn't give to be a deck officer. What he wouldn't give for a little fresh air in the face up on the flying bridge. He knows that sooner or later some German U-boat will take a shot at his ship. The torpedoes usually hit the engine room. Working down there, he doesn't stand much of a chance for survival.

Even before the United States entered the war, the *Modoc* and Wilcox have been under the control of the US Navy and on the so-called Greenland Patrol, escorting convoys, breaking ice, and rescuing survivors from torpedoed ships. They have also been clandestinely tracking German shipping, including U-boats, to support the British navy.

Born in 1914, Wilcox is a 1936 graduate of the US Coast Guard Academy in New London, Connecticut. He has served aboard several ships as both a deck and engineering officer.

A native of Portland, Maine, and Baltimore, he has the fine facial features and slick blond hair of a film-star naval officer. He is the son of a Coast Guard officer who died when Wilcox was in high school. He grew up hearing stories from his father, Lt. Cdr. George E. Wilcox, about being aboard the USS *Morrill* in Nova Scotia

Cadet Robert Wilcox. COURTESY WILCOX FAMILY ARCHIVES.

on December 6, 1917, when the infamous Halifax explosion occurred after a French ammunition ship blew up. The explosion took two thousand civilians and a big chunk of the town with it. Such war stories have instilled in Wilcox a defining alertness and a deep commitment to saving lives anywhere he can.

As the tobacco calms his nerves, his mind drifts to his first taste of naval combat. It came on a dark midnight like this on May 24, 1941. USS *Modoc* and the cutters *General Greene* and *Northland* were picking up crewmen from torpedoed freighters when the *Modoc* found herself on the edge of a deadly battle between Germany's battleship *Bismarck* and the British fleet led by the HMS *Prince of Wales* and HMS *Hood*. At one point Wilcox, coming off duty from his work in the engine room, saw antiaircraft tracers from *Bismarck* flashing over the *Modoc*'s bow. Later, he heard that the *Bismarck* had sunk the *Hood*. She went down in three minutes, taking 1,418 men with her. Only three men survived. The thought of all those men in this icy water makes Wilcox cringe.

⸻

While Wilcox is on Greenland Patrol, Lt. Burtis P. "Pete" Cone's mother Sarah is worried sick about him. He's soon to be the executive officer aboard USS *Leopold*, but at the moment he's serving on a Coast Guard cutter like Wilcox under US Navy jurisdiction. His cutter's job is escorting convoys on the deadly "Murmansk Run" between North America and Russia.

Born to a prominent Richmond, Virginia, family of considerable affluence, this slightly built officer with a devil-may-care grin entered

Peter Cone, officer on USS *Leopold*. COURTESY CONE FAMILY ARCHIVES.

the University of Virginia in 1937. But he lasted less than a year. An avid sailor on Chesapeake Bay and the Rappahannock River, he is a young man in love with the thrill of racing yachts, fast cars, and lovely ladies. After knocking about in the family's manufacturing business for a while and then a tobacco company job, Cone has been rescued from the boredom of a nine-to-five employment by America's entry into the world war. In the cavalier spirit of his ancestors who were Confederate officers, he sees the war as his ticket to adventure . . . and maybe a little glory. It is surely a chance to prove himself to his father, who has grown more than impatient with his footloose son.

Cone tried to volunteer for the Navy, but his asthma disqualified him. Yearning to go to sea, he persuaded his father "Boots" to call a friend to help him enlist in the Coast Guard's officer candidates' program. Now he's the officer on watch and in command of the bridge crew of a Coast Guard cutter shepherding brutally slow convoys along the coast of German-occupied Norway to the arctic port of Murmansk to resupply the embattled Russian army. During 1942 alone, German U-boats have sunk more than ninety ships on this route, a third of which have had no surviving crew. When he's being honest with himself, Cone has to wonder if such losses foreshadow his own future. Then what would his mother think? Would she ever forgive his father for helping him join this war?

One of the men doing the sinking is *Oberleutnant zur See* Erich Harms. Born in 1910 in the Bandt section of Wilhelmshaven on the North Sea, Harms is ancient for an officer on a front-line attack submarine of the *Ubootwaffe*. In fact, he is five years older than his mentor, the captain of U-255 whom he will eventually replace. Behind his back many of the crew refer to him as *der Alter*, the Old Man. This is a common nickname for a U-boat skipper, but Harms is only a watch officer at the moment.

He actually looks old, more like a man over forty than age thirty-four.

Erich Harms, commander of U-255. COURTESY OF DEUTSCHES U-BOOT MUSEUM CUXHAVEN.

He already has tufts of gray hair above his ears. And what ears. Like his long nose, they seem unusually prominent on his thin face. In fact, after nearly two years in combat, his body has the appearance more of a starving refugee than the first watch officer of a combat U-boat. When he smiles, it is just a half smile of the lips with squinting eyes as if he has been staring too long into the sun or witnessed so much death and destruction that true merriment is something he can only recall from another life. His mouth is large and gentle like that of a man who could have been a Lutheran minister in other circumstances, a saver—not a taker—of souls.

Even to his fellow officers like Dieter Hengen, the man who will eventually become his 1WO (first mate), he's a bit of a mystery. Unlike a lot of the U-boat officers, he is not a graduate of the German naval college. He's a reserve officer. He enlisted when the war broke out in 1939. His capable seamanship, close attention to weather and sea conditions, as well as his care with navigation makes his shipmates suspect that he must have come to U-boats after years as a merchant marine officer, but nobody is certain. He never talks about his life.

The truth is that he hails from a family of eleven. Like many of his five brothers, he went to sea early in life and became a deep-sea fishing captain. Many of his officers and men don't know that he has a wife Marie and four daughters back in Bremerhaven. They don't know that the oldest girl Elfriede is just turning ten or that he misses her to pieces. They have no idea how he hates that he has been at sea for so much of his daughters' lives that he seems like a stranger to them when he comes home. He is a voluminous reader, loves fine literature—especially Germany's great writers like Goethe, Schiller, Mann, and Hesse. But he very much enjoys the plays of Shakespeare, the poems of Tennyson, and rereading Homer's *The Odyssey*. More than

once during this war he has thought that he has been on an odyssey of his own, that he is like one of Odysseus's warriors, aging and lost at sea and yearning to return home . . . but doomed to hear the Sirens' call from across the water.

The one thing that Hengen and the other officers of 255 are sure of is that Erich Harms has been single-mindedly fixated on his vessel and her captain Reinhart Reche since joining the crew in November 1941. U-255 has gained a reputation since she went into service as a lucky boat. Reche and this U-boat have been called the "Fox," for their ability to attack convoys and escape her destroyer escorts unharmed. For Harms, Reche has been a

Dieter Hengen, First Watch Officer of U-boat 255. COURTESY OF DEUTSCHES U-BOOT MUSEUM CUXHAVEN.

U-255 at sea. COURTESY OF DEUTSCHES U-BOOT MUSEUM CUXHAVEN.

remarkable teacher. Not only is Reche a capable and stealthy hunter, he has old-school chivalry and compassion. After torpedoing a merchant ship, he gives food, water, and cigarettes to its crew who have abandoned their ship. Then he shows them a course to steer to a safe harbor.

Commissioned just weeks before the Japanese attack on Pearl Harbor, 255 has been sailing out of Norway and raiding convoys ever since. Before the war is over, she will complete an astonishing fifteen patrols.

U-255 at sea. COURTESY OF DEUTSCHES U-BOOT MUSEUM CUXHAVEN.

Harms will forever tell his shipmates, during and after the war, that U-255 is a lucky boat. But he knows that luck has its limits and "lucky" means different things to different people. Still, and without question, this man and this vessel have done and will do difficult things in the name of Deutschland.

Chapter Four

A Place Called Orange

September 1943

Seaman 1/C Sparky Nersasian can't get the taste of ashes out of his mouth or the scent of coal dust from his nose, but he doesn't care. Almost fifty years later he will laugh at the memory of this moment as he tells his niece Tory about standing on the cusp of the biggest adventure in his life.

He's fresh out of gunnery training in Norfolk, Virginia, fresh off a long, slow troop train from Virginia to Texas, with seven Pullman cars plus a baggage car dedicated to the crew of the recently launched DE 319. It has taken days for a series of fuming steam locomotives to drag Nersasian along with fellow gunners Charles "Fran" Bradley and Luke Bobbitt across the country. No matter. Like a lot of the men on this train who are soon to be his shipmates, Nersasian has volunteered for this duty. He was working in a Coast Guard supply depot in Cleveland, and has been so bored out of his mind that he has put in for a transfer to sea duty as a gunner. But what a strange beginning. It has been a hot trip to Texas, and with the windows open in the railway coaches, the smoke from the engines has been billowing over the coasties for what seems like a lifetime. Now here they are. They are off the train. They must find their ship.

The troop train is stopped on a sharp curve, and a couple hundred sailors have poured out with sea bags slung over their shoulders. It's a sultry afternoon, hurricane season on the Gulf Coast. The sky is full of dark thunderheads. The smart fellows in the group are seeking shelter from the heat on the shady side of the Victorian railway station. All the men are looking around them at the flat, sunburnt landscape, the blocks and blocks of frame houses spreading in all directions. Many with asbestos shingles look to have been thrown up in the last year or so. Laundry droops from clotheslines. The roads are dusty and clogged with traffic. Lots of trucks. The air smells of burnt metal, machine oil, and fresh paint.

As US Navy buses roll up alongside the station and stop, someone asks the obvious question. "Where's the ocean?"

"It's a river," says a Marine gunnery sergeant who has stepped off the lead bus. "The Sabine River, swabbies. Welcome to Orange, Texas."

"It looks like the end of the world," says one of the guys with a New York accent. Maybe Harry Daube or Barney Olsen.

"Get your sorry asses on the busses," says the Marine. "Time and tide wait for no man."

⚓

Originally settled by the Atakapas Indians, Orange, Texas, has the natural assets for an industrial hub on this river that divides Texas from Louisiana. Native Americans recognized the advantage of the high bluffs lining the Sabine River and built a community here with fishing as a major source of food and industry. Later, shipbuilding became a natural by-product of a landscape near the Gulf of Mexico and surrounding forests rife with timber for building watercraft large and small.

Shipbuilding here suffered after 1929 and during the Great Depression. Few citizens had jobs. Of the two shipyards on the river, only one had begun steel construction. Wooden boats were still the primary output. Then Consolidated Western Steel Corporation bought sixty-five acres on a bend of the Sabine River and established a fabrication enterprise destined to be one of the largest shipbuilders for the US Navy.

Consolidated's genesis roots in the merger in 1929 of the Llewellyn Iron Works, Baker Iron Works, and Union Iron Works, all of Los Angeles, California. Looking to expand their business, the steel fabricators realized that Orange could supply everything needed for a successful operation: deep-water access, an available labor pool, and a modicum of infrastructure.

Just prior to war in the European Theater, the United States was in dire need of ships. Nazi Germany suspected merchant ships crossing the North Atlantic from the United States of carrying arms, supplies, and personnel and judged them as fair game for U-boats on the prowl. With many losses on the open seas to German U-boats blazing the headlines, public sentiment began to lobby for more warships to protect American merchantmen.

In response to that need, the US Navy assimilated all Coast Guard ships and personnel on October 31, 1941. Sleek Coast Guard cutters, originally painted white to be highly visible for offshore rescue and coastal policing, have been repainted battleship gray and have entered into convoy escort duty, manned with career Coast Guard officers like Robert Wilcox and reserve officers like Pete Cone. But the addition of a few Coast Guard cutters like the *Modoc* on which Wilcox served is hardly enough to deter German U-boats, which have been hunting almost with impunity along America's Atlantic coast.

The navy needs a bigger and modern fleet and Orange is ready. With a huge Navy contract in hand to build small warships, Consolidated Steel has assembled a ready labor force and trained thousands of refugees from Depression poverty to be welders, electricians, fabricators, machinists, painters, draftsmen, and engineers. The shipyard employs approximately twenty thousand workers, and many of the workers are female. With the onset of war, men have been signing up for all branches of service, leaving women to fill the available jobs. The workplace is becoming integrated with both men and women working at the same job. It's a first for this country and demonstrates that women can perform under the same conditions as men and produce quality work. During the shipbuilding boom, the population of Orange has grown from sixty-five hundred people to an estimated seventy thousand. The locals call all the newcomers "boomrats."

At first, these steel warships were launched stern-first, but that technique has proven troublesome with the hulls plowing into the bottom of the Sabine River bed because of its shallow depth. To remedy the situation, hulls are now built on sloped ramps on top of wooden

USS *Slater* (Cannon Class), identical to USS *Leopold* (*Edsall* Class). COURTESY DESTROYER ESCORT HISTORICAL MUSEUM, ALBANY, NEW YORK.

skids. At launch time, the hulls are little more than shells with basic superstructure. Prior to the launch, workers with large buckets of pig fat smear it on the skids to help the hull slide into the river. This process is where the term "greasing the skids" comes from. During the building of the destroyer escorts, the goal is to "splash" a new ship every Saturday. Most of the town turns out for the event. As soon as the ship settles down after the launch, a small tug hooks up to the new ship and tows it to the nearby piers for the final fitting out and the arrival of the ship's officers and men.

In addition to the 149 ships that will be built at Consolidated, Levingston Shipyard will construct 160 barges, troop carriers, and auxiliary ships. Weaver Shipyard will deliver 135 wooden minesweepers designed to evade German magnetic mines. Forty-three destroyers and ninety-two destroyer escorts will be included in the tally of ships built at Orange during World War II. Among those DEs will be a series of six sister ships laid down in the spring of 1943 that are of special interest to Sparky

USS *Slater*. COURTESY DESTROYER ESCORT HISTORICAL MUSEUM, ALBANY, NEW YORK.

Nersasian and his buddies. Those six will become Task Group 21.5 of Escort Division 22. They will be commissioned as the USS *Poole*, USS *Harveson*, USS *Peterson*, USS *Kirkpatrick*, and USS *Joyce*, and they will be manned by crews made up completely of Coast Guardsmen. The one that Nersasian will call "home" will be USS *Leopold*.

Chapter Five

Tin Cans

Spring 1943, Sabine River

SPARKY NERSASIAN WHISTLES, A LONG NOTE THAT STARTS HIGH AND slides down low the way some guys whistle at pretty women.

"Would you look at that?" He's standing with about five dozen other coasties on the riverbank eyeing a long and narrow gray ship tied to a fitting-out pier.

USS *Leopold* launch, June 12, 1943, Consolidated shipyard, Orange, Texas (only ship photo in existence). COURTESY US NAVAL HISTORICAL CENTER.

3"/50 cannon. COURTESY DESTROYER ESCORT HISTORICAL MUSEUM, ALBANY, NEW YORK.

The black letters beneath the haws pipes for the anchor chain say *319*. Launched on June 12, 1943, she will be commissioned USS *Leopold* on October 8 with Lt. Cdr. Kenneth C. Phillips, USCG, in command. The ship's name honors the memory of Ens. Robert Lawrence Leopold, who died aboard the battleship *Arizona* during the attack on Pearl Harbor.

"Feast your eyes, men," says a Coast Guard petty officer. "She's bigger than anything our little service has ever had. You better take good care of her."

"The ship, she is a beauty," Fran Bradley writes home to his beloved "Toots."

Nersasian has grown up in coastal New England. He has seen the fishing trawlers of Gloucester and the last of the big wooden Grand Banks schooners. He has admired their ruggedness and sweet curves. But this ship is beyond anything that he imagined even at gunnery school. It seems twice the size of a Coast Guard cutter and—with that collection of guns—319 looks threatening as all hell.

Coasties Gale Fuller and Bill Miller, two guys who grew up land-locked in the Midwest, have eyes the size of silver dollars.

DE 319 is what World War II sailors have nicknamed a "tin can," for the thin three-eighth-inch steel plates that form the hull. It is one of 563

SEAMAN FIRST CLASS
GALE L. FULLER

Collage of photos showing seaman Gale Fuller in uniform. COURTESY HARRY STILLWELL (FULLER'S NEPHEW).

destroyer escorts quickly built for the United States and its allies to protect convoys from submarine attacks, a true hunter-killer. Nersasian's ship and her five sisters are among eighty-five *Edsall* Class DEs built during World War II. More than thirty of these ships are manned by US Coast Guard crews. She's 306 feet long, thirty-six feet seven inches abeam with a draft of ten feet five inches. Her displacement is 1,253 tons, and she will carry a crew of approximately two hundred officers and men. At flank speed she can steam at about twenty-one knots, thanks to her four Fairbanks Morse diesels. Her range is 10,800 nautical miles at twelve knots.

The *Leopold* has three three-inch/50-caliber deck guns. The ones that Sparky Nersasian sees on the bow will be his special province along with his pals Bradley and Bobbitt. There are two 40mm cannons, eight 20mm cannons, three torpedo tubes, two depth charge racks, and eight depth charge projectors called K-guns. She carries one hundred depth charges ready to launch over an enemy submarine. In addition, the *Leopold* has a hedgehog array, a forward-firing weapon that launches mortar bombs. They explode on contact with a submarine. The brand new DE carries state-of-the-art radar and sonar that can detect a U-boat at up to four

Hedgehogs (USS *Slater*). COURTESY DESTROYER ESCORT HISTORICAL MUSEUM, ALBANY,
NEW YORK.

thousand yards. She is the first and only one of her sisters to be equipped
at this point with HF/DF ("Huff-Duff"), high-frequency direction-find-
ing equipment that can spot, locate, and track an enemy submarine by
listening to its radio transmissions.

For convoy duty, the Navy does not need a full-size destroyer of two
thousand tons, 375 feet in length, with a crew of over three hundred.
Unlike destroyers, the destroyer escorts don't need to be able to steam
at speeds of thirty-five knots to keep up with a task force of battleships
and major aircraft carriers. DEs only require a top speed of slightly
more than twenty knots in order to protect merchant convoys traveling
at between eight and fifteen knots. In addition, DEs can be built in
only three months.

As Nersasian lifts his sea bag and prepares to follow the petty officer
and his shipmates to his berth aboard this sleek beauty, his mind drifts
back to a moment when his troop train stopped in a small Ohio town.

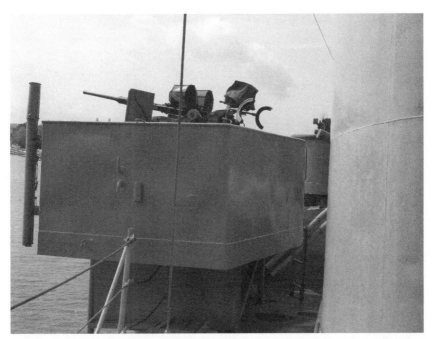

20mm gun (USS *Slater*). COURTESY DESTROYER ESCORT HISTORICAL MUSEUM, ALBANY, NEW YORK.

40mm gun on the USS *Slater* (same as on the *Leopold*). COURTESY DESTROYER ESCORT HISTORICAL MUSEUM, ALBANY, NEW YORK.

3"50 cannon (USS *Slater*). COURTESY DESTROYER ESCORT HISTORICAL MUSEUM, ALBANY, NEW YORK.

Depth charges (USS *Slater*). COURTESY DESTROYER ESCORT HISTORICAL MUSEUM, ALBANY, NEW YORK.

Berthing quarters (USS *Slater*). COURTESY DESTROYER ESCORT HISTORICAL MUSEUM, ALBANY, NEW YORK.

Maybe his shipmates had some premonition about the future, because a strange urgency infected the coasties. They descended on the town's five-and-dime store and bought up everything on the racks. *What was that all about?*

Something stirs in his chest. He feels pride, no doubt, in being part of something bigger than himself, something with a will of its own, something that bonds him to all these other boys in sailor suits. But there is another feeling as well. Something that makes him wish he had a cigarette. He can hear a voice in his head asking, *What have I gotten myself into?*

Lying at an adjacent pier to DE 319, DE 317 is nearly ready for her commissioning ceremony on September 30, and Bob Wilcox is in a pensive mood. He has recently been promoted to lieutenant commander and assigned to be the commanding officer on this ship. It will be named USS *Joyce* after Ens. Philip Michael Joyce, who died in action on February 19, 1942, during the bombing of Darwin, Australia.

Standing on the flying bridge of his ship, he draws on his pipe and

watches the gunner's mates on the two bow 3"/50s talking over the safe storage of live ammunition with a chief petty officer and the quickest way to supply their cannon in battle against a U-boat. Every day he feels like he has grafted his soul to 317 more thoroughly. He knows that he and two hundred other men will have to trust their lives to this vessel. The ocean is a hostile environment. A person's ship is all that stands between a sailor and death. He has seen the remnants of torpedoed merchantmen, been on the scene when the monstrous *Bismarck* sank HMS *Hood*. Life can be hell out there on the deep blue. This ship may have to carry him there and back. *She's my ship goddamn it. Mother, wife, mistress.* If he and his men treat her right, she may just save a lot of lives when the shit hits the fan.

Capt. Robert Wilcox, commander of the USS *Joyce*.
COURTESY WILCOX FAMILY ARCHIVES.

Joyce, *Leopold*, and their sisters are part of what is becoming a proud tradition. Between 1939 and 1945 America will build six successive classes of destroyer escorts. DEs are 290 to 308 feet long with a displacement of 1,140 to 1,500 tons, and a crew of 180 to 220 officers and men. Although they do not have the speed or armament of destroyers, DEs are more maneuverable than their bigger sisters and cost less than half the price to build.

Sailors like Sparky Nersasian on DEs are three-year enlistees in the Coast Guard reserve. They are mostly younger than twenty years old and largely inexperienced except for a few petty officers. Commanding officers like Ken Phillips on the *Leopold* and Bob Wilcox on the *Joyce*, both graduates of the Coast Guard academy, are not much older. Quite a few of the junior officers like Pete Cone have not finished college. But Wilcox is sure that youthful enthusiasm will serve these DE crews well and give them an esprit de corps and can-do spirit.

The problem is that there's a plaintive letter from Wilcox's wife Alice in his cabin. She's still in Florida with their son Richard, staying with her parents. She's worried about his new assignment on this tin can. People say that U-boats have been playing hell with convoys.

Earlier this year the newspapers leaked the story of a slow convoy designated HX228. It left New York on February 28, 1943, as the second of four convoys totaling more than two hundred merchant ships and escorts. German intelligence had broken British codes and knew the locations of the convoys. The Ubootwaffe high command, known as BdU, ordered three wolfpacks of thirty-eight U-boats to lay in wait for the convoys in an area southeast of Greenland not protected by shore-based anti-submarine aircraft. The convoys had their first meeting with the U-boats on March 6-7. The attacks continued until March 19. When the U-boats withdrew, the Allies had lost thirty-three ships and about five hundred men. Only three German submarines were lost.

The freighter *William C. Gorgas* was leading the thirteenth column in rough seas on the night of March 11. At 0242 hours the Gorgas took a torpedo from U-557. The survivors abandoned ship. The sub fired another torpedo two hours later, which detonated the explosives stored in the number-one hold and shattered the night sky. The British destroyer HMS *Harvester* picked up about fifty of the *Gorgas*'s crew, but only twelve survived. The *Harvester* got hit by a torpedo from another U-boat.

"Bob, please be careful," Alice writes. She wants him to put his personal safety first, wants him to put the welfare of their family ahead of his career.

Pleas like this make him sigh. He wishes that he could be a better family man, but he is a man who believes that he is nothing if, above all, he does not do his duty for his men, his ship, his country, and fellow mariners in peril. Ever a student of history, he finds guidance in the words of Adm. David Glascoe Farragut at the Battle of Mobile, "Damn the torpedoes, full speed ahead." This is as close as he comes to having a personal motto. He's a tin can sailor.

CHAPTER SIX

Shakedown

February 1, 1944

"CONVOY IN A HELL OF A MESS." SPARKY NERSASIAN IS WRITING ON A three-by-five-inch card. He's propped on his left elbow in his pipe berth. It's the middle berth in a stack of three. The coastie from Salem is so cold that even in bed he wears his long johns, woolen pants, and shirt. He has been keeping a daily log of his voyage, a new card for each day. He has written over thirty cards since the *Leopold* left Norfolk, Virginia, the day before Christmas. It has escorted a "slow convoy" UGS-28, with over one hundred ships, from the Chesapeake Bay to Egypt and Morocco. The speed of this armada is only about eight knots. Now DE 319, with her sisters *Poole* and *Kirkpatrick*, are part of a task force escorting the west-bound GUS-27 from the Mediterranean back across the Atlantic to America. This convoy seems even slower than the first one, and things aren't going well.

"One ship is spun around. Can't turn because of headwind and seas," writes Nersasian. "Waves are 40 to 65 feet high. Rolls of 45 degrees have been logged. [We are] turning back to look for stragglers."

Man against nature. Thoughts of this struggle bring chills to Nersasian. He used to think the war was about going nose-to-nose with the enemy. But after more than a month straight of dueling with brutal sea conditions, he and his shipmates are coming to the same conclusion as the men fighting for both the Allies and the Axis in North Africa, the Solomon Islands, and Russia this winter. The enemy is an intermittent challenge, but foul weather is a nearly constant monkey on your back.

The crewmen of the *Leopold* are reaching their limit. On another card Nersasian has inked, "All hands in bad mood. Fights springing up from all quarters. . . . Chow lousy. Weather cold." It seems like weeks since anyone could go out on deck. The *Leopold* has been plunging into head seas, burying her bows up to the boat deck in green water. One of his shipmates, maybe Armand Burgun or Harry Daube, has nicknamed the ship the Leapin' Leo. If ever a ship had a "shakedown" cruise, this is the ship and the passage.

To keep from flying out with each pitch and roll of the ship, he wedges his feet and shoulders against the chains that suspend his berth from the one above. Like most of his shipmates, he has been on a self-regimented diet of bread and water for days to hold seasickness at bay. He has heard from some of the guys who have bridge watch that most of the officers are seasick, too, except for the executive officer Lieutenant Cone. Cone, it seems, has spent a lot of his youth sailing small boats. Rocking, rolling, and wiping saltwater from one's face is nothing new to Cone. The guy appears to thrive on adversity. He's only a year or two older than Nersasian and already the executive officer of a warship at sea, while Nersasian has a strong feeling that he will begin and end his sea duty as a seaman 1/C. *Where do men like Cone come from? Does fate mark some of us for glory . . . or do we choose our destinies?*

For a little mental relief from his existential thoughts and the misery of trying to ride the Leapin' Leo through this storm, Sparky Nersasian urges his mind to go back to memories of calmer weather when he still thought going to sea was fun. The nominal shakedown cruises for DE 319 came after her commissioning on October 18, 1943. Except for the surprise hurricane back in July that had struck the Galveston, Texas, area, hurricane season was unusually quiet.

When the *Leopold* ventured out of the Sabine River for Galveston and then on to New Orleans, the Gulf of Mexico was a millpond. Her first extended cruise offshore to Bermuda made Nersasian and his buddies think that they were on a tropical holiday. Sure they tested the guns, practiced with anti-submarine detection gear, dropped depth charges, and fired a torpedo. Lieutenant Commander Phillips went through all the normal routines to shakedown a green crew and a new ship. But what Nersasian remembers are the pink cottages of Bermuda, the palm trees, the pale blue water. He could see starfish and lobsters on the bottom of the harbor at St. Georges from the deck of the ship. He'll never forget his first frothy taste of English stout in a dark pub, his first sweet sip of a rum and Coca-Cola with a wedge of lime served to him on a hotel veranda when he was out on the town in Hamilton with Luke Bobbitt and their gang. When he thinks about Bermuda, he hears the light-hearted passages of Mozart's Jupiter Symphony playing in his head. But then came this convoy duty and the real shakedown. The music playing through Nersasian's brain shifts to the urgency and drama of Beethoven's Symphony No. 3, Eroica. Everything about this storm and war now feels heavy with gravitas and a sense of being caught up in an ageless battle.

As a lover of history as well as classical music, Nersasian knows that the convoy system roots in ancient marine practices. It gained modern acceptance during the Napoleonic Wars. Britain had its merchant ships travel in defined groups to hide and protect them from French warships. When World War II broke out, British merchantmen began suffering 10 percent losses to the German U-boat fleet. In response, England revived the convoy concept. Merchant vessel losses to U-boats dropped to less than 2 percent after England and America began forming ships into tight blocks accompanied by squadrons of escort destroyers. The DEs steam at the vanguard of the ships, patrol the convoy's flanks, and, with slow convoys, cover the merchant ships at the rear as well.

Vessels in convoy travel in five or more columns only a few hundred yards apart. The close formation yields exceptional protection to the vessels at their core. Because convoys concentrate a lot of shipping in a very small area, ships traveling in convoys are harder for predators to find than individual ships traveling known sea lanes where enemy submarines can wait to pounce.

Convoys try to avoid popular routes and, as far as Nersasian can tell, prefer to cloak themselves in weather that makes U-boat attacks difficult. Some convoy strategist and course plotter sitting in a warm office in London, New York, or Washington, DC, must be feeling particularly clever for hiding the *Leopold* and her convoy in this tempest. Seasoned mariners have been calling the winter of 1943–44 the worst weather in the North Atlantic since the start of the war. Misfortune stalked the Leo's eastbound trip to the Med. On December 28 a tanker captain died. On December 30 a ship lost a man overboard. Then a seaman on a freighter died in surgery on January 9. Meanwhile the seas grew heavier. And there was little relief for the crew at Casablanca, where the ship had to limit liberty and double up its guard because Italian frogmen were allegedly trying to plant explosives on Allied warships.

The men of the *Leopold* were eager to escape the dust and heat of the Moroccan coast. But not long after joining the westbound GUS-27 convoy of 108 merchant ships and sixteen escorts, things started to fall apart again. On January 20 the *Leopold* spotted a sub but could not engage it. A tanker captain died of a heart attack on January 22 before a Navy doctor could be transferred to his ship. The only things that got passed to the dead man's ship were nine pints of formaldehyde to embalm his body. Then on January 27 this storm started to rage, and it hasn't let up.

A wave hits with a bang on the starboard bow. The noise echoes through the ship. Nersasian's note cards go flying. The thunder of the breaking sea shudders through the steel ship. She rolls so far onto her port side that men tossed from their berths hang from the chains.

"Oh, geeze," says the coastie from Salem. "And you wanted to go to sea?" He knows that the *Leopold* is bound for New York to join another task group of escorts. The Statue of Liberty will be a most welcome sight.

Fair seas or foul, Fran Bradley has been writing letters to his Dorothy, varying his salutation between "Toots," "Honey," and "My Darling Wife," depending on how homesick he feels, how sad it makes him to think that he has missed Christmas with his young family. "By my absence of letters I presume that you know that the inevitable has happened and I am far away. It has been a long time since we have seen land and we may be sailing to our greatest adventure yet to come." Sometimes he makes oblique references to the last time they had sex. Sometimes he insists that when he comes home they need to get down to the serious business of making another baby. This one he's sure will be a boy, whom he wants to name Patrick Aloysius Timothy Bradley. In his blue moments he writes that he hates missing his daughter Mary Frances's first birthday. "You know, Honey, I don't think I could take this much longer if it was not the thought I was fighting for you. It gives a proud and lofty push. . . ."

CHAPTER SEVEN

Old Wolves

February 26, 1944

THE CREW OF U-255 MUST BE PRAYING THAT HER LUCK WILL HOLD when their skipper Oberleutant zur See Erich Harms gives the order for a course change down the voice pipe and adds, "*Westvärts.*" Westward. It is a rallying cry among U-boat crews, and this boat is going to sea again. The Old Man's tone is even, his speech sure. But he can be anything but certain as he stands on the observation deck of the conning tower, hugs the shoulders of his *U-Boot Päckchen*, leather deck gear, and tightens his checkered scarf around his neck against the bitter north wind.

It's force 4, ten to fifteen knots, on the Douglas Sea Scale. Seas are running four to eight feet with a medium swell. The sky is overcast, but he can clearly see the Marstein lighthouse on a small island bearing 160 degrees. It is less than a half-mile away. The 255 rises and falls in the gray swells under this leaden sky. Her escort the freighter *Unitas*, converted to a heavy arms transport since the start of the war, leads the way at a stately seven knots through the mine fields. They guard the Korsfjorden and the channel to the large *Kriegsmarine* base at occupied Bergen. He listens carefully to the exhaust rumble of the two Germaniawerft six-cylinder diesel engines. They have just been totally overhauled, and he's not sure that they sound right.

This submarine may not be the same lucky boat that entered the shipyard four months ago. She has seven successful patrols to her credit, but now after four months in the hands of ship fitters at Bergen, she might be a can of worms, or what the Germans call a *schwimmen der Sarg*, a floating coffin or a *Schroffhaufen*, a pile of junk. Who knows if members of the Norwegian resistance movement have subtly sabotaged her during her repairs. Such things are becoming common at the U-boat bases in France.

This could be a lonely cruise. Harms's friend, the former first watch officer Horst Selle, has been transferred back to Germany to take command of another U-boat, and many of the old crewmen have been replaced. If that's not enough to rattle the Old Man, there are also the changing odds against U-boats. They have turned distinctly deadly since 255's glory days under her former captain Reinhart Reche. Her chances of coming home are no better than one in five now.

Back in the summer of 1942, when Harms sortied with Reche into Arctic waters on the first of his seven cruises as a watch officer aboard U-255, the U-boat service had been a proud cadre of warriors. Harms felt invigorated and accomplished during those cold patrols in the Arctic seas. He and Reche sunk nine ships, and terminally damaged another, for a loss of over fifty-four thousand gross tons for the Allies. These victories over the enemy have won Reche the coveted Iron Cross medallion and trained Harms to be a capable hunter.

But Reche has moved on. Selle has moved on. And here's Harms still bound to this old boat and heading westward on a two-month patrol south of Iceland. If and when she finishes hunting, she will no longer be going back to Norway, which has been her home for more than two years as a front-line U-boat. She will steer southeast for the 7th U-Boat Flotilla base at St. Nazaire in occupied France, by all reports a hellish place of Allied bombing and French sabotage.

Everything is changing. There was no band on the pier yesterday when the U-boat left Bergen, no strains of the nostalgic folk song "*Muss i' den . . .*" that bands traditionally play when a German warship leaves on patrol. During the earlier years of the war, the "Happy Time" when German submarines ruled the seas, *Konteradmiral* Karl Dönitz was the father of the Ubootwaffe and commander of the submarines, the *Befehlshaber der Unterseeboote* (known as "BdU"). No longer. Dönitz is now the commander-in-chief of the entire navy. U-boat service no longer feels like a select fraternity of comrades in arms. Now, the Ubootwaffe has over four hundred new submarines and twenty thousand new men.

Not many of them are coming back from patrols. In just the last seven months, more than 160 U-boats have vanished beneath the waves. The day will come when a memorial at the base of a tower on the harbor at Kiel will stand in tribute to over twenty-eight thousand men lost in U-boats during World War II. Harms is well aware that England and America have been outbuilding Germany in warships for two years. From what the Old Man has heard in his pre-patrol briefings, British, Canadian, and US anti-submarine aircraft have nearly the entire North Atlantic covered.

In addition to his enemy, Harms faces winter storms and seas that can dwarf a U-boat. But no matter. Even if he's a bit battle weary, it is more than time to get himself and his men away from the beer halls and brothels of Bergen. Time to get away from the immoral stench of a sub-jugated nation where Himmler's SS has set up nine *Lebensborn* camps. Norwegian women are being encouraged or coerced into sexual unions with SS officers to produce blond, blue-eyed, German-Viking children for the master race.

This patrol is only Harms's second since his promotion to being 255's commander back in July, but few U-boat officers have the advantage of being with a single vessel for so long. He has been in this boat for twenty-six months as either second watch officer, first watch officer, or, now, captain. As he follows *Unitas* in his *unterseeboot* away from Bergen and the coast of Norway, he must feel like he and 255 are a pair of old wolves, growing long in the tooth together. He has recently celebrated his thirty-fourth birthday. Not many men are serving on the front lines of a war at his age. It seems a lifetime ago when he was a deep-sea fish-boat captain hauling aboard schools of cod in his nets, a lifetime ago when he and Marie lived in their little home in Wesermünde and their baby girls kept coming one after the other. First, Elfriede in 1934, then Erika in 1937, and Ema, just as he enlisted in the navy in 1939. Precious little Monika was born just last July. He wishes this war had never begun. During the rare times he is on leave to return home between patrols, his daughters look at him as if he is a stranger. He never stops worrying about them in Bremerhaven. It seems like the Allied bombers just keep hitting that city.

Few U-boats have survived as many patrols as U-255. Despite her four-month refit in Bergen, 255, a Type VIIC U-boat, is a hard-used veteran. She is a 568 Type VIIC attack U-boat commissioned between 1940 and 1945, just one in a class of vessels considered the workhorses of the Kriegsmarine, and the most produced submarine design in human history. Shipyard workers laid the keel of this U-boat on December 21, 1940 at the Bremer Vulkan yard at Bremen-Vegesack and launched her on October 8, 1941. *Kapitänleutnant* Reinhart Reche and Erich Harms were aboard for her commissioning on November 21, 1941. That seems a lifetime ago.

Unlike the type IXC long-distance cruiser often assigned to solo patrols on the far side of the ocean, 255 is an attack boat, a sea-going fighter plane, designed to work in wolfpacks of sister submarines that employ hit-and-run tactics against enemy convoys. She is slightly over 220 feet long, with a beam of just over twenty feet. U-255 displaces 757 long tons and has a range of eighty-five hundred nautical miles. Depending on the patrol, her crew numbers between forty-four and fifty-two men. When traveling on the surface, which is most of the time, she is capable of speeds of seventeen knots. But under water she is much slower. Her electric motors only propel her at four knots with a maximum range of eighty miles before her batteries need to be recharged. She has four torpedo tubes in the bow and one in the stern, and she is carrying fourteen torpedoes. In addition, she has an 88mm, quick-firing deck gun and two 20mm antiaircraft guns.

Harms is all too aware that his vessel's basic design derives from World War I–era German submarines and prototypes that evolved in the early 1930s. Back in the early days of the war, 255 and her sisters were effective predators against slow convoys guarded largely by World War I–era escort ships. But the war has exponentially accelerated improvements in his enemy's designs and technology. When he is being honest with himself, when he tunes out the relentless clatter of the diesels, he fears that the Americans' new destroyers and destroyer escorts will prove

Flying bridge on the USS *Slater* (same as on the *Leopold*). COURTESY DESTROYER ESCORT HISTORICAL MUSEUM, ALBANY, NEW YORK.

themselves more than a match for this boat. It is quickly being made obsolete by faster convoys that can travel at fifteen knots and much more sophisticated anti-submarine-warfare gear that the Americans carry. His best hope against US destroyers and escorts is that he carries a new weapon. It's called a T5 "GNAT" torpedo, and it has been designed to home in on the sound of the screws of a destroyer. The trouble is that few U-boats have had experience with the T5 yet.

So . . . who knows? It's time for the deck crew of 255 to wave *auf wiedersehen* to her escort *Unitas*. It's time to shout "Alarm" down the voice pipe and sound the warning bell through the boat that calls the crew to their duty stations for a crash dive. A crew can't practice this maneuver enough. It could save their lives . . . unless this old boat is not up to the stress any longer.

Chapter Eight

The Jitters

March 9, 1944, 0630–1400 Hours

"ALL HANDS TO GENERAL QUARTERS, MR. BALL." LT. CDR. BOB WILCOX has just climbed up to the flying bridge of the *Joyce*. It is 0636 hours. The way he's clipping his words gives a clear indication that he's got a hot agenda. He tells Ball to exercise the depth charge, hedgehog, and gun crews.

Sunrise is just a silvery glow below a deck of scattered cumulus clouds on the eastern horizon ahead. The ship is steaming at seventeen knots with a big bone in her teeth. Visibility is seven miles. The wind is out of the west on the DE's port quarter at force 3 on the Beaufort Scale, about six to eleven knots. Seas are nearly smooth with a westerly swell. The air temperature is 41 degrees; surface water temperature is 45 degrees.

The skipper doesn't give a reason for waking up the half of the crew who were off watch from their precious sleep. As captain of this ship he's not required to give anyone a motive for his orders, but in this case the *Joyce's* executive officer, and the officer of the deck on this watch, Lt. H. G. Ball, already knows what's behind the command. Wilcox wants his crew primed for combat. Ball has read Operational Order #1-44 from Captain Kenner on USS *Poole*, commander of Task Group (CTG) 21.5.

According to the order, the six Coast Guard DEs of this newly constituted task group—*Poole, Harveson, Leopold, Peterson, Kirkpatrick,* and *Joyce*—have been ordered to sail as escorts with Convoy CU-16 on March 1 from New York to Ireland. This is day nine of the trip, and everybody is tense. For most of these men, this voyage is their first high-latitude North Atlantic convoy. In the first paragraph of the order, Kenner has written, "Enemy submarines are very active in areas through which [the] convoy will travel. And attacks can be expected at any time. . . . The utmost vigilance must be exercised."

At the convoy conference briefing before CU-16 left New York, Wilcox heard that England's secret U-boat tracking unit at Bletchley Park, which has secretly broken the Germans' Enigma code, "estimates between 15 and 20 submarines" on a line that passes through 58 N Lat, 26 W Long. This is the area known to Sparky Nersasian and his shipmates as "Torpedo Alley." It is exactly the position that the *Joyce* and CU-16 will reach by nightfall today. To make crews even more on edge, the convoy has already had one U-boat scare. Yesterday, on March 8, USS *Leopold*, using her Huff-Duff gear, got a fix on a radio transmission from a U-boat along the convoy's route. Captain Kenner ordered an immediate alteration in course to avoid the area.

As the sky brightens, Wilcox and the other men on the *Joyce's* flying bridge can see the silhouettes of the twenty-seven ships (mostly tankers) of this high-speed convoy traveling at fourteen and a half knots. *Joyce* has just been ordered to take station three in the fan-shaped escort formation surrounding the convoy. Because she is at station three, the *Joyce* is steaming on the starboard flank of the convoy. It is in seven columns with four ships in the first six columns, and three ships in the seventh. The *Joyce* is sawing back and forth toward the convoy, then away—changing course every three minutes—screening for U-boats with her radar and sonar. By Kenner's order, the *Leopold* has switched places with the *Kirkpatrick* and moved to station five astern of the *Joyce* on the starboard flank from her previous position on the port side of the convoy. The change of the convoy's course yesterday has put the known U-boat on the starboard flank, so Kenner wants the *Leopold* on that side. It doesn't matter that she has the least experienced crew in the task group. Leapin' Leo is the only escort in the group with Huff-Duff to listen for the sub.

When *Joyce* veers away from the convoy, Wilcox and Ball give orders for the guns to fire five or six rounds each off to starboard, making sure not to hit the *Leopold* steaming about 3,500 to 4,000 yards off *Joyce's* starboard quarter. The *Joyce* rattles and booms with the recoiling of her cannons. The scent of exploding gunpowder fumes over the flying bridge. It's still dark enough to clearly see 20mm and 40mm tracer rounds firing from USS *Leopold*. Ken Phillips has his men at General Quarters and his gunners practicing. The crew of the *Leopold* must have the jitters too.

It's about halfway through the afternoon watch when the loudspeaker aboard USS *Leopold* booms, "Now hear this." All personnel not actively engaged in the operation of the ship are requested to assemble on the fantail for a film that reviews abandon-ship procedures.

Rolling out of his second-tier bunk, Sparky Nersasian doesn't like the sound of this. Despite the decent weather, neither he nor his buddies Luke Bobbitt and Jerry Claus on the number two gun crew have settled into their roles aboard the *Leopold* on this trip because of the constant drilling to prepare them for the unimaginable. *And here we go again.* Most of the morning the crew has been practicing offensive combat tactics. Now the captain has decided to prepare his men to play extreme defense. Like surviving Arctic water in early March is even a remote probability? When someone brings up the topic of abandoning ship at a mess table, usually someone else ends it with a remark like "Don't even think about it. Old Adolf's not gonna kill you. You're gonna freeze to death."

Nersasian joined the Coast Guard imagining that he would have a life like the guys at the US Coast Guard Station back in Salem, Massachusetts, who come home for dinner almost every night after polishing their launches, rescuing broken-down fishermen, or patrolling off Marblehead or Misery Island. It seems like serving in the Coast Guard used to be akin to being a fireman: day after day of serene boredom punctuated by rare moments of excitement and a chance to be a hero. But since the Coast Guard came under the wing of the US Navy back in 1941 by an executive order of President Franklin Roosevelt, serving as a coastie has been like being in the blue-water navy for the crews who man thirty DEs. Before the war is over, hundreds upon hundreds of convoys will cross the North Atlantic at the rate of about one a week, many with coastie escorts.

Nersasian might describe the experience of his last two convoys as constant, low-grade fear and annoyance. This convoy has turned up the volume on his emotions a few more notches. It seems like this trip has been drill, drill, and more drill. He hasn't had a good sleep since leaving New York on March 1. But although it feels more than a little bothersome to be roused from his berth to go watch a training film, "You never know when you might learn something, right?" That's Nersasian's attitude.

Like his father who escaped the killing Turks in Armenia, Sparky Nersasian wants to be the fellow who is ready for anything. Jack Dempsey's boxing instructors back at Manhattan Beach pretty much beat survival into him. He feels tough, fit from all the boxing and PT workouts. And he's gotta thank the Champ for teaching him to keep up his guard both literally and figuratively. *Semper Paratus.* That's what the tattoo on his bicep says. But ready for what exactly? He would give up a month's pay to know that.

Chapter Nine

Torpedo Junction

March 9, 1944, 1715–1755 Hours

THE VOICE OF THE RADIOMAN, THE *FUNKER*, INVADES THE WARDROOM like something from another world. The Old Man and one of his officers have been sipping ersatz coffee after their supper of sausage and potato stew at a tiny table.

"*Was?*" asks one of the men. What?

The Old Man has been rolling his hot coffee around in his mouth and imagining better days nestling next to a warm fire with a mug of hot *glühwein* at his home in a district of Bremerhaven. At least he can be glad that the food is still fresh and that the dinner sausage was not laced with a soybean filler called *Bratlingspulver* that the Ubootwaffe has begun adding to the tinned foods sent out on patrols. But it's cold in the boat. Except within five feet of a few space heaters, the temperature in 255 is about the same as the water that surrounds the boat, about 42 degrees. Harms is wearing his hat with its white tropical cover and a thick, roll-neck Norwegian sweater. No doubt he's wishing that the beard he started when he left Bergen was coming in faster.

"*Kontak, Herr Kaleun.*" The voice of the hydrophone operator (*Unter-wasserhorchoffizier*), known as the *Horch O*, booms again over the deep hum of the boat's electric motors. The voice is firm, without emotion, as it announces a sound contact on the boat's hydrophone array. *Herr Kaleun* is U-boat slang for Kapitänleutnant.

U-255 in Norway early in the war before modifications to the conning tower. COUR-
TESY NATIONAL ARCHIVES OF NORWAY.

Harms bolts to his feet and heads a few steps aft of the wardroom
for the Horch O's cubicle to grab the headphones and listen for himself.
For the moment he can walk without being thrown against a bulkhead.
It's calm when the boat is running submerged like this, working her way
westward at four knots, 160 feet below the surface.

Much of the patrol so far has been through waves of fifteen to
twenty-five feet. On the surface, the U-boat has seen rolls of up to 60
degrees in these seas because she has grown top-heavy with the weight
of added antiaircraft guns and ice. Even in moderate seas she rolls 30
degrees. There has been so much vomiting aboard 255 that the men have
been masking the smell by leaking a little diesel oil from the fuel filter

drains into the bilge, by cooking greasy sausages at almost every hour of the day, and by dousing their bodies, clothes, and pillows with Muelhens 4711 cologne. The Ubootwaffe has sent 255 to sea with cases of cologne to mask the wretched smells a U-boat develops on patrol. Some of the men in the forward torpedo room, often called the "House of Lords" on U-boats, have been saying that their quarters smells like a particularly sordid brothel that they know in Bergen.

Harms should not be surprised by the Funker's call. Only six hours ago he got a message from BdU: "Harms join Group Preussen and occupy with economical transit speed AK 3869 as attack area."

The German navy has divided the world's oceans into a grid of large, lettered boxes, 486 nautical miles per side, with smaller numbered boxes within them. AK 3869 is about four hundred miles south of Iceland along the 58th Parallel. It's the place that the Americans call Torpedo Junction. For the first three years of the war, this same area was known as the "Air Gap" because it was too far off shore for Allied anti-submarine aircraft to patrol. But now with air bases in Iceland and long-range patrol bombers like the American PBY and B-24 as well as the British Sunderland seaplane, the Allies have closed the Air Gap. Brilliant searchlights on the newer planes have made it dangerous for U-boats to run on the surface at night as well as during the day. Just a few days ago 255 barely escaped a Sunderland on anti-submarine patrol.

But air cover or not, 255 will be hunting in Torpedo Junction as she joins the wolfpack called *Preussen Gruppe* in search of convoys. And things look promising. Harms is just arriving on station and already his Horch O has picked up the beating of a ship's propeller. The Old Man has never been here before. All his previous patrols have been in the Arctic, but he has heard that Germany has sunk more than fifty Allied ships in this area, and he is hopeful that he can claim at least one more victory for the Third Reich despite his aging boat.

What is the bearing?

The Horch O says he has a *Horchpeilung*, a sound echo, at 290 degrees relative to the 255.

"Up to periscope depth," he tells the engineer as he ducks through an open hatchway into the control room, the *Zentrale*.

He tells two petty officers to pass the word that brings the crew to their battle stations. He does not shout the traditional warning, *Alaaaarm*, nor does he ring the bell that calls the men to General Quarters with an incessant jangling. This evening he wants his boat running as quietly as possible. The enemy is surely near and has gotten very good at listening for the telltale sounds of a U-boat. Only stealth can save the *untersee* fox's life.

"Bearing 300 degrees now," says the Horch O into his voice pipe.

Harms is in the conning tower with his hands on the arms of the attack periscope. He's sweating despite the cold. It takes deep breathing to calm himself. Since the first contact twenty minutes ago, the Old Man has seen nothing. The glow of the setting sun blinds him as he tries to search to the west of 255 through both the sky periscope and the attack periscope. But there is definitely a ship out here, somewhere. Finally, he surfaces for a look around. Despite fifteen miles of visibility, he could see nothing because of the final flaring of the setting sun, then the sudden darkness of the winter night. So he has taken his boat down again with hopes that the hydrophone operator can get another clear sound bearing without the distortions from the U-boat's bow wave while running on the surface. And now, at last, the Horch O has locked in the ship. It's in position to cross 255's bow in a few minutes. Three questions rise in the Old Man's mind. Is it the enemy? Should I take a shot? Or should I be the "shadower"?

The shadower is one of the key players in a wolfpack. U-boat wolfpacks operate according to a process that Grand Admiral Karl Dönitz calls *Rudeltaktik*, the tactics of the pack. Like pack animals such as wolves, U-boats often depend on group dynamics to subdue prey that is larger and traveling in greater numbers. The shadower is like a wolf scouting ahead of the pack until it spots a herd of prey. Its job at this point is to alert the pack and track the prey. When the pack arrives, the wolves attack the herd in a way that strikes fear into the group as a whole and leaves some individuals isolated and vulnerable to injury or death by the wolfpack.

Submarine wolfpacks and Rudeltaktik date back to the German U-boat force at the end of World War I. Seeing their effectiveness against convoys, Dönitz has made the wolfpack a primary operational formation for many submarine patrols in World War II. Before the war ends, Germany will send out over 250 wolfpacks to hunt Allied shipping, with usually three to twenty submarines in an individual wolfpack. The usual protocol for the wolfpack is for the individual U-boats to spread out on a line more or less perpendicular to the anticipated route of the convoys, with the boats spaced at about 30–40 nautical miles from each other. When one of the U-boats detects a convoy, it follows the convoy unseen and radios BdU of the convoy's position and direction. BdU in turn radios all the members of the wolfpack with the information so that as many submarines as possible can convene on the convoy and attack when there are enough U-boats to overcome the threat of the escorts.

Once the pack is on scene for the attack, individual captains can pick their own targets and devise their own strategies for outmaneuvering the escorts and sinking the merchant ships. Many commanders prefer night strikes, firing fan shots of multiple torpedoes from more than a thousand meters off a convoy's flank. A few favor head-on daylight rushes into the middle of the convoy while loosing their explosive "eels."

In the Happy Days of 1941–42, wolfpacks lost very few U-boats while sinking thousands of merchant ships. But the tide has turned since May of 1943. Bletchley Park has cracked the Enigma code. Massive Allied air coverage of the North Atlantic and astonishing improvements in the American and English sonar, radar, and Huff-Duff have put U-boats at a distinct disadvantage.

U-225 is participating in the very last and the largest wolfpack to hunt the North Atlantic. Formed on February 22, 1944, it will hunt until March 22. During this time more than thirty U-boats will move in and out of the pack. The hope of BdU is to cause such devastation and chaos with Preussen Gruppe that the Allies will be so busy fighting the Battle of the Atlantic that they will not have the weapons or manpower to mount an invasion of German-occupied Western Europe this coming spring. But the effects of this wolfpack will be minimal. Preussen will sink only five ships for a total tonnage loss of about fifteen thousand tons while losing eight U-boats. This wolfpack's failure will cause Dönitz to largely abandon Rudeltaktik and start relying more heavily on lone wolves.

But Harms knows none of this as he wrestles with his choices—to shadow or to attack. All he knows is that he needs to see this ship. He and the Horch O believe it is an enemy steamer traveling solo. But he needs to verify this supposition with his own eyes before he makes a decision. He checks the boat's clock and sees that it is 1755 hours. According to his almanac the moon should be up and nearly full. Maybe by its light he can spot his prey. Then he can confirm that it is an enemy vessel and decide whether to attack or to shadow.

If he has stumbled across a convoy, he knows that he will be the only U-boat in the area for at least two hours even if BdU were to call in the pack. By listening to BdU's messages to other U-boats, Harms knows that U-986 is about thirty miles away. He cannot wait for her. His many patrols with Reinhart Reche have taught him that this is the moment to be bold. If he remains underwater, the steamer will soon outrun him.

"Blow the ballast," he calls down to his *LI* (*Leitender Ingenieur*) in the Zentrale. Then he zips up his leather jacket and tightens the checkered scarf around his neck as he prepares to open the deck hatch. "Take her up again . . . and arm all eels."

CHAPTER TEN

On the Edge

March 9, 1944, 1915 Hours

"Now hear this. All hands secure from General Quarters."
The order to stand down from battle stations echoes over USS *Joyce*'s
PA system.

Lt. (jg) John Bender of Princeton, New Jersey, wishes he could
breathe a sigh of relief, but he can't. There has been no rest for the weary
today. The captain has ordered a call to General Quarters on three of the
last four four-hour watches and required gun, depth charge, and hedgehog practice on each watch. But while the third call to General Quarters
is over for the day, Bender doesn't feel relieved.

He's juggling too many things on not enough sleep. Not only is he
the OOD (officer of the deck) in command of the *Joyce* from the flying
bridge at the moment, but he is also the ASW (anti-submarine warfare)
officer on the ship. His boys in the sound hut on the flying bridge and in
the CIC (Combat Information Center) room below on the O2 deck have
been having a hell of a time. The SL radar that scans for surface targets
in CIC has been acting up since leaving New York, and a technician has
been fiddling with it nearly constantly just to keep it up and running.

In the last few days it has become clear that the ship's anti-submarine
sonar in the sound hut has problems too. There seems to be a water leak—
that is getting worse—in the dome receiver mounted on the bottom of
the ship. The leak is causing what the sonar operators call "water noise,"
a rumbling sound that blanks out all return echoes on the sonar when

Sound hut on the USS *Slater* (same as on the *Leopold*).
COURTESY DESTROYER ESCORT HISTORICAL MUSEUM, ALBANY, NEW YORK.

the boat is going over fifteen knots (which is most of the time). Even at slower speeds the sonar only seems to be able to get return echoes from large targets within two thousand yards. At any speed at all water noise completely drowns out echo returns coming from 315 degrees to 360 degrees off the port bow. If there is a U-boat out here, the *Joyce* may well not be able to hear it or see it.

It's dark and all the ships in the convoy are blacked out. From the flying bridge Bender can only sometimes glimpse the shadows of the ships in the convoy heading eastward toward Ireland. He sees the shadows off to port when the rising moon breaks out from behind cirrostratus clouds. He knows that the *Leopold* is zigzagging somewhere off his starboard quarter at thirty-five hundred to five thousand yards, but damned if he can see her. The wind is blowing about fifteen knots and seems to be picking up. He can see the silvery flashes of breaking seas. Everything looks blurry. One has to hope that the lookouts can see more.

Lt. Cdr. Wilcox has been resting on the berth in the day cabin behind the steering station on the O2 deck. No doubt he will be checking in

Sound hut on the USS *Slater* (same as on the *Leopold*).
COURTESY DESTROYER ESCORT HISTORICAL MUSEUM, ALBANY, NEW YORK.

with Bender at any second to see how the last General Quarters drill went, and Bender, the ever-conscientious prep school grad of prestigious Phillips Exeter Academy, wants to be on top of his game for his captain. Maybe coffee will improve the OOD's night vision. Maybe it will wake him up. All he can do is call down to the galley for another mug of hot Joe and hope for the energy to see his watch through to 2000 hours . . . then he can get back to the sound hut and CIC to check on how his sonar and radar operators are making out.

Down in CIC Norwegian-born Barney Olsen, the Staten Island boy who became a coastie without the benefit of proof he had US citizenship, is standing at his SL radar unit. The CIC room is almost dark except for the green glow of electronic screens and the light over the plotting table. Olsen's peering down at a six-inch screen that gives range and bearing to surrounding targets. He's watching the green line that represents the rotating antenna sweeping around the screen about once every three seconds.

The range is set on twelve miles, but on his screen he can hardly see the convoy off to port or the *Leopold* less than three miles astern. He keeps trying to fiddle with the gain control on his unit to try to tune out the sea clutter from the breaking waves. But changing the gain settings only occasionally renders a clear image of the ships around the *Joyce*. If Mr. Bender were to appear right now and ask him how goes the fight, he might be tempted to call a spade a spade—"regular snafu, sir." This thirteen-hundred-pound unit, the size of a refrigerator, needs to go to the radar hospital for serious rehabilitation.

The US Navy coined the acronym RADAR in 1940 to stand for RAdio Detection And Ranging, but radar is still emerging from its infancy in March 1944. England, Germany, the Soviet Union, and the United States were working on radar technology throughout the 1930s, creating devices that transmit radio signals and measure echoes coming back from targets. But the big breakthrough came in 1940 when John Randall and Harry Boot of Birmingham University invented the cavity magnetron. This device made it possible to send and receive micro-wave-band signals that allow for the detection of even small objects at sea like a U-boat periscope.

In September 1940, England shared the cavity magnetron with the United States, hoping that American R&D and manufacturing capacity could make ship and airborne radars a nearly immediate reality. In response the US government funded the Radiation Laboratory known as Rad Lab at MIT to advance radar technology and bring competent systems to ships, planes, and early-warning, land-based stations. Eventually four thousand people will work in the Rad Lab, and about half of the radar used in World War II will originate from there.

When it's working well, SL radar can detect a large ship at twenty-three miles, a surfaced submarine at eight miles, and a periscope at two miles. But tonight on the *Joyce*, Barney Olsen has few kind words for the engineers at their lab on the Charles River in Boston. What if there is a U-boat out here? With all the clutter on his screen, could he see the enemy in time to warn the convoy? He sure as hell has to hope that the guys on the other DEs like the *Leopold* are having better luck at the moment with their gadgets.

PART TWO
INTO THE FRAY

CHAPTER ELEVEN

Shadows

March 9, 1944, 1942 Hours

COLD SEA WATER SOAKS THE WHITE COVER OF THE OLD MAN'S *SCHUL-mütze*. The peaked officer's cap is pulled down tight on his head as he flings back the tower hatch cover on U-255 and boosts himself off the aluminum ladder, through the hatch, and onto the tower observation deck. He barely notices the water running in rivulets over his ears, his cheeks. Wet heads are commonplace for a U-boat skipper who is often the man opening the tower hatch cover after a submersion . . . and besides he has bigger things to worry about than a little dripping water. U-255 has been tracking a ship now for almost three hours. In that time Harms has brought his boat to the surface twice before but has not seen the target. This time the target seems closer. It's his duty to not let it get away.

Heading 020 degrees to intercept the eastbound ship, the boat is rolling heavily in beam seas as two seamen on the watch detail clamber out of the hatch. Harms has to grab the pedestal-mounted UZO (*Underwasserzieloptik*) for balance. He hopes that soon he will need it for more than just keeping himself upright. He hopes it will be the tool to score his first victory as a U-boat commander. He has brought this old boat a long way across a hostile ocean for this chance.

The UZO has two parts, a set of large, heavy binoculars and a rotatable bracket set in a degree-marked ring. It's linked to a mechanical analog attack computer called a *Vorhaltrechner* in the U-boat's conning tower, which sends attack headings into the torpedo launch receiver in the forward and after torpedo rooms and to the guidance system of loaded torpedoes.

For this surfacing, Harms has handpicked the two seamen joining him on the tower because they are veterans of earlier patrols and have the best eyes in the boat for spotting enemy ships. A bank of clouds obscures the moon at the moment, leaving just the faintest glow on the sea. But as the Old Man wipes the dripping water from his face, one of the lookouts says that he sees a shadow bearing 350 degrees. Before Harms can bring the shadow into focus, the lookout says that it has turned away, is gone.

The Old Man unplugs the voice pipe and calls down to the Zentrale, "*Auf Gefechtsstation.*" Battle stations.

The men on the tower of 255 see nothing for several minutes. The sea and sky have darkened until the boat seems wrapped in gloom and failure. But then the clouds sail off to the west. The rising full moon turns the seas to a sheet of beaten silver. Off to port Harms can clearly see the silhouettes of ten to fifteen ships perhaps three or four miles to the northwest. Many appear to be tankers.

"*Schiffe,*" ships. One of the lookouts says the obvious.

"*Amerikaner,*" says the other by way of identifying the shapes.

Instantly, Harms realizes that he has not been tracking a lone freighter as he has imagined. He's looking at a high-speed convoy that is traveling at close to fifteen knots . . . and he is exactly in the wrong position to shadow it or attack. Not only is the convoy going so fast that he can only keep pace with it at nearly flank speed, but the convoy is between the rising moon and 255. In this position the enemy escorts might see him clearly painted by the light of the moon.

He wonders what his former captain Reinhart Reche would do. The Fox would say that probably the Americans will spot him visually or on radar before he can get close enough to acquire a target with the UZO, program the Vorhaltrechner, and fire a fan shot of three torpedoes. His best chance is to try to circle behind the convoy and to shadow the ships from a position where 255 will be harder to see. Once he is in a safer position to disappear, he can risk sending out a KTB radio message to

U-boat command and have them call in the wolves. This could be a glorious victory for the Third Reich . . . but he must make his move immediately or the convoy will soon be out of reach to the east.

He calls down the voice pipe to the battle helmsman. Turn left, "*Bachbord.*" The boat saws left as Harms issues a new heading. Something dark and large looms off the port bow.

CHAPTER TWELVE

Contact

March 9, 1944, 1930–1957 Hours

A FIVE-PIECE BAND—INCLUDING A TRUMPET, A CLARINET, AND A GUITAR— are jamming to the Mills Brothers song "Paper Doll" in the *Leopold*'s midships berthing compartment as gunners Sparky Nersasian and Luke Bobbitt prepare for a cold night on deck. They are about to relieve the crew on the ready gun fifteen minutes before the official watch ends. It's the custom on warships. The men are putting on boots, jungle pants, jackets, and woolen watch caps as they savor the hot licks of a clarinet solo.

They are still bantering about bars, beer, and broads they plan to conquer when the ship gets to Ireland in a week as they head up to the boat deck and the ready gun. It's dark and cold as hell when they reach their gun, but moonglow starts to break through a cloudbank. They can see sea smoke blanketing the water. It's an eerie night, and it puts Bobbitt in mind of a disturbing movie he has seen called *The Most Dangerous Game*.

Bob Wilcox jerks awake, sits up in bed. Someone is knocking urgently on the door of his day cabin on the bridge of USS *Joyce*.

"Skipper, sir, *Leopold* has a radar contact bearing one nine zero, eight thousand yards." The voice is John Bender's. He was just being relieved as the OOD at the end of his watch when the message from the *Leopold* came in over the TBS, Talk Between Ships, radio. "*Leopold* is investigating."

Wilcox is already on his feet, running his fingers through his hair, looking for his winter coat. "Call the ship to General Quarters, lieutenant."

He has been nervous all day, fearing a U-boat attack. He has been so on edge that before falling asleep for the last two hours he reread the procedures for avoiding live torpedoes fired at his ship. But now a strange calm is settling over him. There's no more time for worries. Duty calls. The time is 1950 hours.

"I have the con, Mr. Bender," he says, sliding into his coat, grabbing his life vest and heading for the flying bridge. And just like that, he's in charge. He knows that whatever happens now is totally and forever on his shoulders.

⚊ ⌢

An alarm sounds and the PA system on USS *Leopold* booms, calling all hands to General Quarters. Seaman/1C William J. Miller is reading a magazine in his bunk when the alarm echoes through the crew's berthing area aft of the engine rooms aboard the Leapin' Leo.

"Captain wants you on the flying bridge, Miller. Move it." A petty officer is in his face. Miller doesn't panic; he doesn't think about his parents or his two younger brothers, Jerome on a destroyer and Ervin with the Navy in England. He just thinks it's going to be cold as hell tonight on the flying bridge. He's the captain's talker and he could be up there in the bitter wind with Lieutenant Commander Phillips for God knows how long. He's got on his summer underwear but the heaviest socks he owns as he slides into denim dungarees, a chambray shirt, jungle-cloth winter coat, foul-weather jacket, and a woolen watch cap. He grabs his gloves and kapok life vest as he pushes his way through a host of men dressing for winter and battle. He can hear the ship's Fairbanks-Morse diesels beginning to roar, can feel the bow rise with the ship's speed. This sure as hell isn't like the boring old days before becoming a coastie when he was driving a truck back in Pontiac, Michigan. Tonight he might be going toe-to-toe with the Jerrys.

On the bridge he puts on his headphone and mic, hears the radar guy in CIC saying that the target is now at four thousand yards. He tells the captain, Ken Phillips, then checks in with the repair parties. They report

Two forward guns (USS *Slater*). COURTESY DESTROYER ESCORT HISTORICAL MUSEUM, ALBANY, NEW YORK.

"Condition Able," ready as they can be. Meanwhile the captain is calling for his radar talker to send up relative bearings and telling the lookouts to train their binoculars dead ahead. At one point Phillips tells his TBS operator Chief Ben Kinnard to broadcast to the CTG (Commander Task Group 21.5), Captain Kenner on the *Poole*, in plain English. Every ship in the escort group can hear it. "This looks like the real thing."

Kenner fires back over the TBS an order to his six DEs. USS *Joyce* will assist. Everybody else hold your positions.

Chapter Thirteen

Attack

March 9, 1944, 1958 Hours

As the *Leopold*'s crew scrambles to their battle stations and the ship pounds through the seas at twenty-one knots, Sparky Nersasian thinks it's more than strange that just a few minutes ago he was picturing Bobbitt's grand plans for getting them drunk and laid on liberty. Now the ship's general alarm has sounded and things are starting to get hairy.

Nersasian, Bobbitt, and their usual crew of gunners were just relieving the watch on the ready gun when the call came to report to General Quarters. Because seas regularly break over the bow of a DE on North Atlantic duty, the ready gun, which is always manned, is the number two 3"/50 on the bow end of the so-called "boat deck," a level above the number one gun that's generally getting drenched down on the main deck.

Nersasian's job on the gun is to be the pointer. He makes the gun go up and down. He's also the man who fires this cannon. On the other side of the gun is Jerry Claus, the trainer, who makes the gun go left and right. Behind these two men is the gun captain, Fran Bradley. A shell-hander, Zombie, is also working the gun along with Bobbitt and another guy. Two of these men fetch the ammo from the gun-clip room. The third man will toss the empty shell casings overboard.

The 3"/50-caliber deck guns like Nersasian's have been staples of the US Navy since 1890. During World War II, these weapons remain the essential gun armament on destroyer escorts, submarine chasers, mine-sweepers, and some submarines. These guns are also secondary armament on many larger ships. Nersasian's gun fires a projectile that is three inches in diameter. Each shell weighs about thirteen pounds. The barrel of his gun is 50 calibers (twelve feet, six inches) long. The whole gun weighs seventy-five hundred pounds and can fire antiaircraft, surface combat, and illuminating star shells depending on the needs of the ship.

Ready for action, Nersasian and Claus have harnessed themselves into their metal seats on either side of the gun. They have peep sights and wheels to control elevation and the direction of fire. Bradley stands behind them at the back of their gun where he can view a target through an optical telescope and get messages over his headset about radar and visual bearings from CIC and the flying bridge. Bobbitt, Zombie, and the other shell handler await his orders.

When the crew is in synch, they can fire twenty rounds per minute to a maximum range of 12,000–14,600 yards. But nobody is in synch at the moment. The Leo is pitching like a hobbyhorse. Waves are rolling over the deck, throwing spray onto the gun crew. Bradley keeps shouting "Say again" into the microphone that connects him to CIC and the bridge. "Submarine, dead ahead?" "Fire what?" "Star shell?"

⸺ ⸻

An instant after Bobbitt has loaded the star shell into the gun breech, Bradley taps Nersasian on the back. It's a signal. He hits the solenoid firing button and lets the star shell fly. It breaks overhead in the cloud deck off the port bow. The sky, more than the sea, lights up.

Bradley is shouting into his microphone again to CIC, peppering the night with questions. Then he pauses for some seconds, listens. The gunnery officer Mr. Garside is reaming him out. He barks at Bobbitt to load another star shell on the double. And this time could Nersasian and Claus please aim the fucking gun dead ahead and a little lower? The captain's pissed. There's a sub somewhere in the gloom right out front, and he wants a goddamn Fourth of July party overhead. "Fire."

⸺ ⸻

"Submarine," says the *Leopold*'s executive officer Mr. Cone. "Dead ahead." He's on the flying bridge.

63

The *Leopold*'s Captain Phillips orders Seaman 3/C Armand Burgun on the signal bridge to man the carbon arc light, train it on the sub.

The U-boat is crossing the bow right to left at about seventeen knots. She's pulling a big, silvery wake about a thousand yards ahead.

The skipper and his talker Miller see the sub too. "Open fire," says Phillips to his gunnery officer, "Flank speed. Prepare to ram."

The message comes down to the number-two gun crew, and Nersasian thinks, "Holy Cow. This is it."

Babbitt slams a standard, armor-piercing shell in the breech, locks it. Nersasian can't see the sub. He sets the elevation to Bradley's command, then fires. The gun booms, recoils about a foot.

"Jerry, what happened?" Nersasian asks the trainer.

"I think you hit the son of a bitch."

Bobbitt loads the gun again. They fire. The 20mm guns on the port side of the *Leopold* open fire. Nersasian can hear the poc, poc, poc of the twenties hammering away.

———

From the flying bridge of the *Joyce*, Bob Wilcox can see the star shells lighting the sky ahead and the tracers sparking low over the water as the *Leopold* opens up with all her port side guns. She's about six thousand yards ahead, 10 degrees off the *Joyce*'s starboard bow. "Can you see the sub?" he calls down to CIC. Like Ken Phillips on the *Leopold* he double checks to make sure that the FXR gear is deployed. It is a collection of mechanical noisemakers towed behind the ship to distract and confuse the guidance systems of acoustic torpedoes like the Germans' new T5.

After Wilcox hears that the FXR gear is out, he asks a quartermaster to check the degaussing coils to make sure they are reducing the magnetic field of the ship. The coils are a hedge against German mines and magnetic guidance systems in some torpedoes. Finally, he lifts his binoculars up to his eyes and tries to follow the *Leopold*'s tracers to the enemy. Where is that son of a bitch?

CHAPTER FOURTEEN

Fight or Flight

March 9, 1944, 1959 Hours

"*ZERSTRÖRER*," SHOUTS ONE OF THE LOOKOUTS. A SINGLE-STACK destroyer. It's at 10 degrees off U-255's bow and turning toward the sub, distance one thousand meters.

"*Alaaarm.*" Erich Harms is bellowing into the voice pipe, calling for his engineer in the Zentrale to initiate a dive.

As two star shells burst overhead, the lookouts are already dropping through the tower hatch. Gunfire erupts from the destroyer. Harms can see the tracers, can hear the buzz of projectiles overhead as the boat starts to lean into its dive. This is bad. The destroyer is coming on like an angry Valkyrie. *Scheisse.* It could be on 255 before the boat is barely underwater. Harms needs to buy himself some time.

He calls for the crew to fire the T5 GNAT in tube II. It's his best chance. There is no time to program solutions into one of his conventional eels in tubes I, III, or IV.

"The flap is closed," says someone on the other end of the voice pipe.

"*Verdamit.*" He swears into the pipe, tells the torpedo men to reopen the doors on tube II. Do it now. Set the firing data. He just guesses: bearing zero degrees, fix firing angle zero degrees, distance six hundred meters, tube II, T5, depth four meters.

"*Folgen.*" Shoot the damn thing. The destroyer is dead ahead. "Crash dive," he bellows as he drops through the hatch into the tower, pulls the hatch shut with a loud clang, and locks it. Dive, dive, dive.

Below, all the men from the stern of the boat are charging through the Zentrale like a troupe of wild monkeys, trying to get their weight into the bow, trying to accelerate the dive. Trying to avoid being mauled by the American Zerströrer from hell.

"*Los*," calls the first watch officer. Loose. The T5 is on its way.

———

The 255's crew feels the jolt as the pneumatic pressure in torpedo tube II expels the T5 from the port bow. The Old Man orders, *Macht schnell*. Fast. Take her down fast.

Harms rushes down the ladder to the control room. He's counting seconds, wondering if this new anti-destroyer torpedo has a prayer of saving him from the charging American above. At this close distance he expects to know his fate in about thirty seconds. The *Aal*, the eel, will either find the destroyer or disappear into oblivion. Maybe, just maybe, the T5 will work better than the shit for eels that he and the Fox had to deal with early in the war.

Torpedoes have gotten so much better in the last year. Recognizing that its steam-driven torpedoes from the 1920s, with their bubbling wakes, were not stealthy enough for a modern war, the Kriegsmarine developed a battery-driven electrical torpedo known as the G7e powered by a hundred horsepower electric motor and lead-acid batteries. The first versions of this torpedo had a failure rate of between 20 and 40 percent. While the electrically driven torpedoes have the advantage of stealth over the steam eels, the electric Aals have had persistent problems with both types of detonating systems the Ubootwaffe has been using.

The good news for Harms and his U-boat tonight is that engineers have made significant improvements in Germany's eels during the last year. The T3 version of the G7e in tubes I, III, and IV runs faster and farther than the previous designs. The eels have a redesigned detonator that uses the magnetic field of the target ship to explode the warhead. If the eels connect, their target is most likely doomed.

The T5 that is sprinting toward the enemy has been hailed by some of Grand Admiral Dönitz's staff as a wonder weapon. Electrically driven like other G-7 torpedoes, the T5 has a range of fifty-five hundred to six thousand yards and a speed of twenty-four knots. The weapon uses a passive acoustic homing system to find its target. The homing mechanism steers the torpedo on either a circular or zigzag course until it homes in on the sound waves of ship propellers.

But Harms has heard that one problem with the T5 is that it might decide to double back and lock onto the propeller noise of the U-boat that fired it. As a hedge against such a mishap, engineers have set the torpedo for an initial straight run of four hundred meters to allow the U-boat firing it to get away from the eel. Still, Harms has heard T5s have sunk at least two U-boats that have fired them in the past four months. His best assurance is to dive below sixty meters and go completely silent after firing the T5.

The weapon has been in the fleet for a little more than six months so far, and U-boat command briefers have told Harms that the T5 has had some success against convoy escorts. But he has met no other captains in Bergen who have used the weapon successfully. He has also heard rumors that the Russians have captured a T5 and that Britain and America have already designed countermeasures to elude the T5's homing system. So . . . who knows if this Aal can do its duty?

Time will tell. Another twenty seconds more or less. *Achtung*: silence in the boat.

The Old Man races to get 255 to a safer depth below sixty meters. Everyone aboard is counting the torpedoes' run in his head. *Fifteen, sixteen, seventeen* . . . everyone in the boat can hear the churning of the destroyer's screws echoing through 255's pressure hull as the American ship storms toward them. Everyone hopes *not* to hear the high whine of the T5 turning back toward them.

The Old Man knows he must make his boat invisible. If the T5 misses the destroyer, it will come looking for him with hundreds of depth charges and hedgehogs and maybe another escort or two. The U-boat's slipping beneath eighty meters of ocean, the counters are tallying twenty-seven seconds, when the crew feels the boat shudder. Heavy thunder echoes in the forward torpedo room and rumbles aft through the boat. The sound of the destroyer breaking up less than six hundred meters ahead is so loud that some men cover their ears to block out the wailing of a ship ripping apart. The sounds are nothing new to Harms. But he has never heard them at such close range before, and he already knows that he's going to hear these screeches and moans in his dreams as long as he lives. Veteran submariners will tell you that you never forget your first kill, never forget that feeling that only you and not your enemy will live to fight again . . . even if it is just for a few more minutes.

Chapter Fifteen

Hit

March 9, 1944, 2000 Hours

THE MEN ON THE FLYING BRIDGE OF THE *LEOPOLD* NEVER SEE THE TOR-
pedo, never hear the torpedo explode. Not the captain's talker Bill Miller.
Not Ben Kinnard on the TBS nor signalman Armand Burgun at the
carbon arc light. Not skipper Ken Phillips. Not his exec Pete Cone. Not
the gunnery officer Frank Garside in CIC either. One second they are
in the midst of a gallant attack, preparing to ram the enemy and watching
their 3"/50 and 20mm tracers homing in on the U-boat's conning tower.
The next second U-255's T5 blasts in from the port side at twenty-four
knots and detonates almost directly underneath them.

The carbon arc light that Armand Burgun has been training on the
submarine explodes and throws him across the signal bridge. He can feel
himself bleeding from shrapnel wounds to his abdomen and leg. Everybody is lying in a heap on the deck. Bill Miller has fallen on top of the
captain. Now Phillips is trying to push Miller off.

"We're hit," says a sailor.

"No shit."

"Everybody okay on the bridge?"

"I can't see," calls someone.

"Power's out."

"No, I *really* can't see."

"We got no communications, captain, sir." One of the talkers is waving a dead headset in the air.

Despite his wounds Burgun is back on his feet. Phillips tells him to go find Lt. (jg) George Ayrault, the damage control officer, and get a report. Someone hands him a flashlight. Meanwhile Miller and others are still crawling around in the moonlight on their hands and knees, keeping their heads down because they think that the flying bridge got hit by a shell from the U-boat's deck gun. They can already feel the ship starting to sag beneath them as if she's starting to fold up on both ends and they are on the hinge. Some of them must already sense that the Leapin' Leo has suffered worse damage than an artillery hit. She's come to a nearly dead stop and has started a peculiar rolling in the waves. The night echoes with low groans, the screech of tearing steel, the shouts of men.

———

Luke Bobbitt has just loaded the fifth or sixth shell into the number two 3"/50, and Sparky Nersasian is trying to adjust the elevation of the gun to compensate for the pitch and roll of the *Leopold* when "Bang. Explosion." His ears ache, and he thinks, *I'm never going to hear another sound in my life.* Then he realizes that his headset has gone dead. There's no communication to the gunnery officer in CIC. All the power to the gun has gone dead too. He looks over his shoulder to the gun captain Fran Bradley, sees Bradley mouth the word "fire." The firing solenoid has failed, but down by Nersasian's foot is something that he thinks of as a clutch pedal. It's long and wide and out-of-the-way. He mashes it and the round goes flying. He hopes like hell it hits the U-boat . . . because the sub sure as shit got the first lick in. When the torpedo hit, the concussion sent Bobbitt flying headfirst into the breach of the gun with a live shell in his hands. Nersasian can see that the explosion threw up some of the deck grating. It hit Bobbitt in the side of his leg. The man is hobbling as he pitches the live shell overboard.

"Oh, Christ, Jerry," says one of the gunners.

Nersasian unbuckles from his harness and sees that the trainer Jerry Claus is bent over in his seat, still strapped to the 3"/50. He can't talk, is barely moving. The left side of his face is slick with blood. His shipmates unbuckle him and lay him down on top of a case of shells.

"We got to go down below and get life jackets," says Bobbitt.

Nersasian thinks about his wallet, his money, and the three-by-five cards in his trip journal. He'd like to get those things too. But he can picture the destruction below decks. Guys are dead down there, no question. It's pitch dark. And judging by the way the bow is already rising out of the water and twisting to starboard, the lower decks must be flooding fast.

"Are you crazy?" he asks Bobbitt.

But down the hatch they both go into the forward berthing area in search of life vests. The water is already above their knees.

When Armand Burgun finds the damage control officer the news is not good. The torpedo struck the ship in the most-forward of her three engineering spaces. The backbone of the *Leopold* is broken and there is a hole in the port side from frames fifty-eight to seventy-five. The hole extends ten or fifteen feet aft nearly to the bulkhead between the forward engineering space B-1 that houses two of the diesels and the middle engineering space B-2. The cavity goes from below the waterline up through the main deck and includes damage to the superstructure. There is a smaller hole on the starboard side. With the hull skin and at least seventeen frames compromised, the ship is in danger of breaking in half along the expansion joint between the ship's mast and exhaust stack. A watertight door has been blown open allowing water to start flooding the aft end of the ship. This is not what Burgun wants to hear, not what any sailor wants to hear . . . especially in March . . . on the frigid North Atlantic . . . at night . . . with the wind rising.

At the number two gun with the wounded Jerry Claus and the bow starting to rise and twist oddly away from the rest of the ship, Fran Bradley is no doubt contemplating his next move. He's a good swimmer. Maybe this is his time to prove it. But like so many of his shipmates who jump off the bow into the floater nets, he doesn't know how cold water can shock a person's system, how floater nets can act like snares to drag you under, how the life belts that many of the men are using can slide out of position and hold their heads underwater.

71

CHAPTER SIXTEEN

Bump in the Night

March 9, 1944, 2002 Hours

JUST A SHUDDER. THAT'S ALL THAT SEAMAN 3/C JEREMIAH BOWEN feels. He's at his battle station with the Repair 3 gang in the after crew's quarters. A watertight door on a hatch to the after motor room swings open and water starts pouring in. Men had been going in and out of the hatch to get their gear as they rushed to their battle stations. The last man must not have dogged down the door sufficiently. Now the door can't be closed. The lights have flickered out. All anybody can hear is the rush of water starting to flood the compartment. It's dark as hell until someone snaps on an emergency light.

"When it hit, it [the *Leopold*] seemed to stop immediately as if it had hit a brick wall," Bowen will tell the board of inquiry when they call him to testify about the attack on the *Leopold* a month later in New York. The chief in charge of Repair 3 orders his men to head back to the fantail to check the after steering station as it damn well might be needed to steer the ship. But when the crew gets there, they find that the hatch to the steering station lies buried in shoring timber that has fallen against it. The repair gang scrambles to clear away the lumber and finally get through the hatch to man the after steering apparatus. The gyrocompass is out of order and all radio communication with the bridge is dead.

"Somebody better check on the bridge," says one of the gang.

"I'll go," says a seaman. The man is out the hatch, never to be seen again.

Seaman 2/C Gale Fuller has been at his battle station for five minutes, manning the number six K-gun depth charge launcher on the fantail and watching shipmates stream the FXR torpedo decoy gear overboard. He has just set his depth charges on the K-gun at Pattern Baker, detonation at about 250 feet, when the U-boat's T5 rocks the *Leopold*. He can't understand the sudden, sharp roll of the ship. He goes to look over the starboard side for the cause when he gets hit in the face and shoulders by a blast of spray coming over the top of a 40mm gun. Instantly, he's drenched. He's trying to wipe the saltwater from his eyes when an officer orders him to set all of the depth charges back on safe.

When he's done with the depth charges on the starboard side of the fantail, he goes over to the port side and helps set the depth charges on that launcher to safe too. He knows that when an order like this comes, the shit has really hit the fan. The officer fears that the ship may go down and the armed depth charges explode as it does. He can't help his curiosity so when he's done making the depth charges safe, he slips away to walk forward along the port gangway to see what the hell is going on.

A hatch is open and he looks down into an engine room. There's a light on down there. The emergency generator must have kicked in, and he can see that the compartment is a shambles of gear and broken machinery. Water is flooding the compartment. There's no sign of life down there . . . or death either. The scene is so still and calm, he can hardly believe that this is what a disaster looks like. No exploding ordnance. No shouting or screaming. No broken and bloody men. No bodies or body parts. Just the quiet, relentless trickle of water and the heavy scent of fuel oil.

It sounds like a car going fifty miles per hour hitting a tree, thinks Seaman 1/C Harry Daube when the torpedo goes off. He has just taken his battle station as the pointer on the number three 3"/50 gun near the stern of the ship when a gale of water smacks him in the back and the lights go out.

What the hell? That's what he keeps asking his shipmates.

"Torpedo," says someone.

He hears that the engineering officer, Lt. (jg) Kenneth Nelson, and a machinist's mate, William Henry Clark Jr., have been killed. This is bad. That's the word passing around the thirty-five or so men on the fantail.

———

When General Quarters sounds, Seaman 1/C Robert E. Chandler Jr. is coming off watch in the wheelhouse. He runs back to the after berthing area along the starboard side of the ship to snag his life vest. On his return trip to his battle station on gun two, he stops to help another shipmate dog down the hatch to the berthing area. He's hearing a 3"/50 and some 20mm cannons pounding away, wondering what in all heck is going on. A sudden but slight jarring throws him a step forward before he catches his balance against the superstructure. He's thinking that maybe the forward guns are having some kind of target practice until a sailor comes out of the starboard hatch. The boy is bleeding around his face and head. Another fellow's helping the guy, basically holding him up on his feet.

Chandler runs over to the two men, assists the uninjured man in dragging the wounded seaman indoors, in this case, into the head. They sit him down on the floor next to the toilets and send another man to find the pharmacist's mate. The lights are out. The chief motor machinist appears like a goblin in the moonglow and hands him a flashlight to hold while the pharmacist's mate bandages the wounded guy's head.

"I've got another wounded man on the fantail," says the medic by way of telling Chandler to stay with the bandaged guy.

Chandler starts telling the wounded man to relax, stay calm. Everything is going to be okay. The lights will probably be back on in a minute. All this is nothing more than the usual shit show that comes with winter escort duty in the North Atlantic.

But the bandaged seaman seems out of his mind. He keeps asking what's happening. What is goddamn happening?

"We just took a Kraut torpedo," says a guy bursting into the head. "Jerry got us. He got us good."

Electrician's Mate 3/C Herbert Schwartz was lying in his sack fully dressed when he heard the call to General Quarters. Now, he's at his newly assigned battle station in the forward mess deck. His only job is to shut off three valves to the refrigeration room. He does his duty and sits down on a bench wondering why the guns have started pounding away, shivering the Leo. Suddenly, the lights go out and he feels himself going airborne.

He lands like a crab on his hands and feet. He can't see shit and starts groping around in the dark for some clue about where he is. This is only the second or third time that he has ever been in the forward mess deck. He's not one of the sailors like Sparky Nersasian and Luke Bobbitt who has been with the *Leopold* since her commissioning back in Texas. He joined the ship in New York after her convoy to Casablanca.

This is a hell of a mess. He has no idea how he's going to get out of here. Then he hears the creaking of a steel hatch and sees a shaft of faint light, like moonlight maybe, breaking through from above. There's a hatch up there and one of the other fellows who was in the forward mess here is climbing up through the hatch.

Something tells him that if he wants to live, he better follow that man. On the double.

CHAPTER SEVENTEEN

Abandon Ship

March 9, 1944, 2005 Hours

IT'S ALL JUST SCUTTLEBUTT, A RUMOR, AT THIS POINT. THAT'S WHAT SEAMAN 2/C Chester Piechal was thinking . . . at first. He was in the forward 20mm clipping room passing out ammo to the gunners. Now the lights are out, the PA system is out, the radios are out. Everything is out. The ship is stopped dead in the water, and someone is shouting that they just rammed a U-boat.

He wants to see for himself so he goes out on deck and circles around the number two gun. Nersasian and Bobbitt are nowhere to be seen, but Fran Bradley is kneeling next to Jerry Claus who is stretched out on an ammo case. Bradley is talking in low tones, trying to soothe Claus who has a hand pressed to the side of his face. The hand is covered in blood.

What the hell happened?

One of the gunners tells Piechal that he's pretty sure the Leo just took a Jerry torpedo. The front half of the ship, from the bow to just behind the flying bridge and the mast, is rising and falling in a strange way, kind of twisting off to starboard, starting to lean over more and more with each roll of the ship. The air still stinks with the sharp scent of gunpowder.

Someone says that it looks like pretty soon everybody is going to have to swim for it.

Piechal is glad that he's already wearing a bulky kapok life jacket, not a dinky life belt, not one of the inflatable vests. And he's really glad that he

USCG *Harpoon* magazine: the sinking of USS *Leopold*, published April 15, 1944.
COURTESY US COAST GUARD TRAINING STATION, MANHATTAN BEACH.

USCG *Harpoon* magazine: the sinking of USS *Leopold*, published June 15, 1944. COURTESY US COAST GUARD TRAINING STATION, MANHATTAN BEACH.

(Newspaper clipping:)

Leopold Survivors Credit Manhattan Beach Training Life Saving Aid

In one of the first survivor's stories of the sinking of the *U.S.S. Leopold*, manned entirely by a Coast Guard crew, two former Manhattan Beach men credit the saving of their lives to a large extent to training received in "boot" here. The destroyer-escort, the first announced sunk thus far, went down in the North Atlantic 10 March as a result of an underwater explosion according to Navy Department Communique No. 511.

They are Richard Forrester, Torpedoman 3c, of St. Mary's, Pa., and Nelson Nersasian, Seaman 1c, of Salem, Mass. Each survivor, now in Company 44, credited a different phase of his MBTS training for his being alive today.

Nersasian believes that the physical conditioning received in C.O.T.P. training had much to do with his being able to swim to a life raft in the freezing waters. Forrester, who floated in the water an hour and a half before finding a raft in the darkness of night, felt that he was able to remain calm and conserve energy because of things he learned in an "abandon ship" training film seen here.

Both men were reporting for their section watch when the explosion occurred. "In true Coast Guard style everyone was calm. No one lost his head," according to Nersasian.

"Upon orders to abandon ship," he related, "I climbed over the side and down the nets. I had quite a distance to swim to the raft. I was a clerk in civilian life and never was very strong. But I was built-up physically in boot training in the

Manhattan Beach gym classes. I was a bit dazed but a buddy, Lee Bobbit, seaman first, aided me on the raft. It was cold but we sang songs and prayed and tried to keep in good spirits for several hours before we were rescued.

"After a couple of hours on the raft, we were feeling kind of low. One of our buddies saw a chair

floating toward us. It's legs had twisted up until they formed a cross. He called to the other men, 'Look, a good omen!' It gave us a lift. It was only a short time later when we were picked up," Nersasian added.

Forrester was still aboard when the ship sank beneath him. "When at Manhattan Beach as a boot, I

didn't pay too much heed to the 'abandon ship' training film I saw. I didn't until the time we had to use some of that information. Then it all came back to me like a flash," he stated with a snap of the finger.

"When I found myself floating in the ocean, I tried to think of what I should do to save myself. I remembered that the training film said to float on your back as much as possible, so that's what I did at the time. Water and oil went into my nose when I hit the sea, but when the life jacket brought me back to the surface, I quickly remembered to float on my back. I stayed that way about an hour and a half and finally got pulled onto a raft," Forrester concluded, averring he felt fresh despite his experience.

Nersasian said that he also recalled from the "abandon ship" training films that you should get overboard to the windward side and he instinctively did this.

Forrester's family is in all branches of the service. Brother Robert is in the Army infantry somewhere in England, brother Chester is in the Marines somewhere in the South Pacific and sister Helen is a Yeoman 2c in the Waves stationed at Hunter College.

Forrester was in Company 29 in boot training at Manhattan Beach. Two others from that company served aboard the *Leopold* with him—Carl Hofert and Orville Martinson, both torpedomen 3c. Nersasian was in Company 17 at Manhattan Beach. Three others in his company also served on the *Leopold*—Almo Musetti, Walter Spinning and Walter Selivonchick, all seaman 1c.

Richard Forrester, Torpedoman 3c, and Nelson Nersasian, Seaman 1c, former MBTS Boots, photographed in reunion here after surviving sea tragedy—sinking of "USS LEOPOLD" last March.

USS *Leopold* survivors Richard Forrester and Nelson Nersasian in *Harpoon* magazine, published April 15, 1944. COURTESY US COAST GUARD TRAINING STATION, MANHATTAN BEACH.

doesn't have to go below in the dark and hunt for life jackets like Nersasian and Bobbitt. But he wishes he had dressed more for the weather. All he has on over his long underwear is a cotton shirt and a pair of denim dungarees. He's cold just standing out here with Bradley and Claus.

Torpedoman 3/C Richard Forrester had been at his battle station at the number seven K-gun on the fantail. He had just set his K-gun to launch a pattern of thirteen depth charges when the ship seemed to jump right out of the water. Then it settled, and a wave of water rolled over the fantail. He had to hang onto a piece of superstructure called the "arbor" to keep from being washed overboard.

Now the stern has popped back up. It seems higher out of the water than normal and, looking forward, Forrester can see that the center of the ship looks lower. The sea seems to be just about level with the main deck. Someone is shouting about a man overboard. One of the men on the K-guns back here got swept away, but when Forrester looks out at the North Atlantic he sees nothing but moonglow illuminating sea smoke rising off restless waves.

He hears men calling one-to-another to abandon ship, but there are no officers around, and there is no official confirmation. Still, it is pretty clear from the way that sailors have begun to scramble around the ship that he is no longer needed at his battle station. Being a torpedoman, he decides he should beat it up to the boat deck and check on his "fish" in the torpedo launcher. There are three of them. Two of them should be armed and ready to go as is standard protocol when the ship is at General Quarters and in attack mode, but the fish that's in the number two tube has had problems and is down for maintenance. When he gets to the launcher, which is nearly midships on the Leo, he sees that at least one of the Mark 15 torpedoes is halfway out of its tube. The head of it is lying on the ready-service box of 20mm ammunition. This isn't a good thing. It took one hell of a wallop to break this torpedo out of its tube. Each one of these fish carries 825 pounds of explosives, and this launcher is very near the expansion joint in the ship, the weakest point. If the *Leopold* breaks in half, it will be here. There could be hell to pay if one of these steel monsters goes off.

—◦—

At the number two gun, Sparky Nersasian and Luke Bobbitt have returned from the flooding crew's quarters with life jackets. Nersasian goes to Jerry Claus to give him a life vest and Bobbitt asks, "What's the sense of putting a life jacket on him. Look at him."

For the first time since the explosion, Nersasian really takes in the pointer. He appears to have lost half his face—cheek and jaw gone. He's staring at Nersasian with a blank look as if he doesn't recognize him. Nersasian puts the vest on him.

"Come on, Jerry," he says. Nersasian remembers what he learned from the abandon ship film that he and his shipmates watched during the afternoon. Time to get a move on it before all the life rafts are gone.

Claus just sits on the ammo crate and doesn't move.

"Come on, Jerry."

Claus grabs him and won't let him go.

—◦—

Seaman 1/C Glyone Mahaffy was at his battle station as the talker on the 40mm director when the torpedo hit the *Leopold* with a muffled thud. A wave rose over the director and washed him through the shield of the director and along the boat deck.

He staggers to his feet, finds his headset, and tries to contact the bridge. But the communication circuits are out. He takes off his heavy rubber galoshes and heads back to the 40mm gun to see if he can help. All of the gunners are still at their stations awaiting orders, but they are saying that the gun doesn't work. It's out of power. After a while the gun captain says that they should release the life rafts. Mahaffy helps release a life raft and a floater net (to support swimmers) on the port side, but then the gun captain tells him this isn't his abandon-ship station, and he better go find it.

He does, but when he gets there the raft is gone and the ship is already starting to come apart. He can hear the tearing of steel and feel the shudders under his feet. He crosses over to the starboard side of the ship to look for anything there that he might cling to if he has to go in the water, but he sees nothing. Things are starting to feel dicey. Looking forward he sees thirty-five to fifty men beginning to gather on the bow and looking desperate. But what really rattles him is that he sees two torpedoes that have come out of their launcher. They are lying against the ship's exhaust stack, looking like immense bombs. Meanwhile, within feet of the torpedoes, the ship is starting to bend in half along the expansion joint in the boat deck. The joint is there to help the ship flex in a seaway, but now it seems like a zipper about to pop open.

On the flying bridge the skipper Ken Phillips and Bill Miller have become untangled. He hears the captain say he thinks they got hit by a big shell then asks the exec Cone, "Where are we hit?" Miller tries to talk on his headset, but everything is dead. Someone asks him where his life vest is. It's in the sound hut, he says, and goes off to find it. In the sound hut, he's surprised to see that the place is empty. Where in hell did everybody go? When he comes out with his vest, the skipper and the rest of the bridge crew have already left.

About the same time Herbert Schwartz has popped up from the mess deck through the hatch into the wardroom, which is a jumble of toppled furniture. It's only a few steps out onto the boat deck. Here he runs into Pete Cone the executive officer, who seems to be inspecting the ship's damage. Cone is handing him a lit battle light to secure when Schwartz sees the captain come out of the ship's office carrying a bag. Neither of these officers is wearing a flotation device.

Someone asks, "Is it true we are supposed to abandon ship, sir?"

"Just a minute," says Phillips. He looks aft along the boat deck, sees the buckling around the expansion joint, maybe sees the torpedoes lying against the stack. "Abandon ship." His voice sounds steely. "All hands, abandon the ship. Pass the word."

The 40mm director operator Seaman 2/C Warren Young has just gotten the order to abandon ship and is heading from his battle station to his abandon-ship station at life raft number two when he sees the loose torpedoes. A month later back in New York he will tell a board of inquiry, "They were smoking or steaming a little bit."

No one then, or for the next seventy years, will give Young's observation a second thought.

CHAPTER EIGHTEEN

Going Deep

March 9, 1944, 2006 Hours

ERICH HARMS CAN NO LONGER HEAR THE CRACKS AND SCREECHES coming from the destroyer overhead, maybe because his heart is pounding and his blood is humming in his ears. But not hearing the American doesn't mean that he isn't there, doesn't mean that he isn't licking his wounds and collecting himself for a depth charge attack. And even if he's mortally wounded, he will have at least one other *Feger*, sweeper, backing him up. That's how escort groups work. Harms has to get his boat away from here. Hit and run. This is the tactic that he has learned from his mentor Reinhart Reche. This U-boat can't run fast underwater, only four knots, so she has to go deep. The Old Man tells his engineer to open more vents in the ballast tanks. Take 255 deeper, faster. Take her to what the Ubootwaffe calls "depth 2A." Take her to 160 meters, 590.5 feet.

Maybe she can get below a thermocline that will mask her from the enemy's sonar. It's a risk. The design-depth of a Type VII U-boat is about 180 meters. Harms and Reche have taken 255 deeper, but who knows if she still has the strength. She's been through a lot since 1941. Her recent refit in the shipyard in Norway could have changed everything, not necessarily for the better. Damn diesels have begun to run rough already on this patrol.

Harms orders the boat to rig for silent running. Then he asks his officers and chiefs in the Zentrale to tell the men to prepare for *Wabos*. It's their nickname for *Wasserbomben*, depth charges. Aboard 255 on September 23, 1942, the Old Man lived through an attack by an RAF Catalina patrol plane that seriously damaged the boat with two depth charges and forced her return to Norway. Since then, depth charge attacks scare the hell out of him. Maybe it's memories of that attack by the Catalina that make him so cautious, even to the point of being a restrained eater. He knows that the American DEs can release a dozen Wabos at a time on an enemy submarine. Each of the US Navy's Mark 9 depth charges packs two hundred pounds of Torpex explosive. Crews can set the Wabos to explode to depths as far underwater as six hundred feet. Each destroyer escort carries about one hundred depth charges. There are surely two destroyers up above. That means they could rain down hundreds of depth charges on 255. It's a nightmare in the making.

But survival is possible. U-boats have escaped horrendous barrages of depth charges. One boat during the war will claim to have survived over six hundred Wabos. Depth charges damage submarines by creating a water hammer effect. It radiates through the sea after the charge explodes. The lethal radius of a depth charge depends on the depth of detonation, the amount of explosives, as well as the size and strength of the U-boat's hull. A depth charge like a Mark 9 has a killing radius of only three to ten yards against a Type VII U-boat. But a Mark 9 can wound a sub at thirty yards. This is what Harms always fears from a depth charge attack, what most of the men in the Ubootwaffe fear. Instant death may be the slamming of a door on life. But being in a wounded boat stuck on the bottom while your shipmates slowly suffocate or drown around you, that's a nightmare that brings on a terror that the crews call *Blechkoller*, tin fright.

The alternative to suffocating on the bottom of the sea is no better for the crews of mortally wounded U-boats. In 1939 Adm. Karl Dönitz sealed their fates when he issued War Order #154 to the Ubootwaffe. His intention was to bring an end to the chivalrous practice of rescuing enemy combatants after a torpedo attack. During World War I U-boat commanders often picked up the crews of the merchant ships on which they preyed or gave the shipwrecked sailors lifeboats, food, water, and directions to safe harbor. No more. In War Order #154 Dönitz asserted a take-no-prisoners policy, which reads in part:

Do not rescue any men; do not take them along; and do not take care of any boats of the ship. Weather conditions and proximity of land are of no consequence. Concern yourself only with the safety of your own boat and with efforts to achieve additional successes as soon as possible. We must be hard in this war. The enemy started the war in order to destroy us, and thus nothing else matters.

In 1942 Dönitz doubled-down on his take-no-prisoners policy with what is known as the Laconia Order:

All efforts to save survivors of sunken ships, such as the fishing out of swimming men and putting them onboard lifeboats, the righting of overturned lifeboats, or the handing over of food and water, must stop. Rescue contradicts the most basic demands of the war: the destruction of hostile ships and their crews.

The orders concerning the bringing in of captains and chief engineers stay in effect.

Survivors are to be saved only if their statements are important for the boat.

Stay firm. Remember that the enemy has no regard for women and children when bombing German cities!

Harms is all too aware that if this is the way that German submariners have been ordered to treat their enemy, he can hardly expect the crew of an enemy Feger to treat him and his men differently. If a Feger drives him to the surface, he expects no mercy.

As 255 plunges deeper, the hull moans from the depth. The needle on the *Tiefenmesser*, the depth gauge, passes 150 meters. The sub must get out of the reach of the Mark 9s. If the destroyers' sonar finds 255 before she is below about 190 meters, this could be a very short game of fox and hounds. And if this U-boat makes it deeper than the service range of the Wabos, how long before the sea crushes her or she has to come up for air? A Type VII like 255 that has just crash-dived after only a brief period on the surface for air and battery charging has little breathing air or battery life. Twelve hours is what Harms and his crew figure.

It's standing room only for about thirty men crammed into the forward torpedo room so that their weight in the forward end of the boat aids 255 to accelerate her dive. And accelerate it does. For men like first watch officer Dieter Hengen, it feels as if they are on a downhill charge from one of Norway's peaks in a runaway sleigh. The newcomers in the crew grit their teeth against the groaning of the pressure hull, against the ever-increasing cold penetrating the boat from the deep water outside. They feel a knot in the guts. They gasp for air. The stale scent of their shipmates' fear and the ordinary rank odor of a U-boat makes them want to gag. The 255 stinks of fuel oil, fried sausage, armpits, garlic breath, fake coffee, intestinal gasses, and *Scheisse*, shit. The House of Lords is a cramped pipe full of chain falls, immense torpedoes, and anxious boys. A few ceiling bulbs cast the scene in dim shadows.

What makes things worse, what makes these sailors bite their lips and pray, is the knowledge that for the last ten months of this war things have been going very wrong for U-boat crews. The crews keep track of the boats that leave and come home. But it is something that these men never dare talk about. Since May of 1943 the Ubootwaffe has lost more than twelve thousand young men from a service that will total fewer than forty thousand seamen over the course of the war.

They know that while the destroyers overhead are the immediate threat, at some point the escorts will have to rejoin their convoy. And at some point they will call in anti-submarine aircraft from Iceland, the "bees." These days the bees are responsible for sinking three out of every four U-boats that are lost. Deadly American-built B-24 bombers, equipped with sophisticated magnetic detection gear, sonar listening buoys, powerful searchlights, and sharp, new radar have joined the ranks of the Catalinas and Sunderlands based in Iceland. The British and Canadian squadrons flying out of Iceland call their B-24 bombers LRVs. They can carry up to eight thousand pounds of anti-submarine bombs or depth charges and patrol to a distance of one thousand miles from their bases. Quite possibly the escorts hunting 255 have already called in the LRVs to help with the attack. If a swarm of these bees finds 255, they can hound her until she has to surface. Then they will bomb or depth-charge her to hell.

Harms would like to send a radio message back to BdU telling U-boat command that he has spotted a convoy and giving its position. BdU could call in Preussen Gruppe. An all out attack by ten or fifteen U-boats would bring a desperately needed victory for the Fatherland. It would also, no doubt, infinitely increase U-255's chance of survival . . . if she can evade the escorts until the wolfpack gets here. But Harms suspects that by sending a message now, the chances are extremely high that the enemy's Huff-Duff will locate him and make him food for fishes in short order. He has not survived so many patrols in this U-boat by being hasty so now he restrains himself, just as he holds himself back when the steward places a plate of food in front of him on the wardroom table. He will wait before breaking radio silence.

What he doesn't know is that he is safer than he fears. The only ship in the escort group overhead that carries Huff-Duff is the USS *Leopold* . . . and she is dead in the water and breaking up. With Bob Wilcox and the *Joyce* charging in to aid the *Leopold*, Convoy CU-16 only has four escorts to protect her and could be easy prey for a large wolfpack like Preussen Gruppe . . . if only the sea wolves knew.

Maybe another U-boat commander would send out a KTB message to headquarters and call in the pack right now on CU-16 at the risk of losing his boat and his men. Maybe another skipper would risk everything to give Hitler and Dönitz the victory that they sorely need to distract the Allies from their plans to invade Western Europe this spring. But Harms has been fighting the good fight for almost three years now. He is too old, too war-weary, and too cautious to sacrifice himself and his men for the glory of a dying government. No one can say that 255 has not already done her duty for the Third Reich tonight. So . . . he keeps his boat's radio quiet as it plunges toward some of the deepest canyons in the North Atlantic. Like his enemies in the *Leopold* and the *Joyce*, Harms must feel that he's caught in a knife fight in the dark. It will be hours before anyone besides the crews of these three boats really knows what happens here.

Chapter Nineteen

No Response

March 9, 1944, 2008–2014 Hours

On the flying bridge of the *Joyce*, Bob Wilcox is feeling the frigid wind burn his cheeks and wishing he had his pipe. Not because he thinks the smoke will warm his face and chest, but because it calms him. He's a man who always looks cool and collected to his crew, but they don't know the tensions that rocket around inside his body behind this mask of bravura. They don't know that he's sometimes so intense that the only things that can keep his hands from shaking are a pipe-full of his Heines Blend or a stiff drink. Occasionally, when he's ashore in places like New York with other officers like Pete Cone from the *Leopold*, there are too many stiff drinks.

The *Joyce* is charging to intercept the *Leopold* at twenty-one knots. Peering through his binoculars, Wilcox still can't see her, but his CIC talker reports that radar has the Leo about 6,000 yards ahead and slightly off the *Joyce*'s starboard bow. USS *Joyce* is closing fast on her sister ship, but the ASW officer John Bender says that his men in the sound hut can't hear anything on the sonar, not even the beat of the *Leopold*'s props. Bender and his minions can only hear the rushing roar of "water noise" from the sonar dome. The leak appears to have gotten worse. Perfect. Just goddamn perfect. *Joyce* is storming into battle deaf.

A few minutes ago Wilcox was squinting into his binoculars, watching the star shells and tracers flying from the *Leopold*, thinking, *This is how it begins.* He knows. He remembers again that night on May 24,

1941, when he was on the *Modoc*, rescuing crewmen from torpedoed freighters and the German battleship *Bismarck* started shooting anti-aircraft tracers across the *Modoc*'s bow. That was the night that the *Bismarck* struck the HMS *Hood*, the night that over fourteen hundred British seamen abandoned the *Hood* for the icy water and only three lived to tell about it. A goddamn nightmare. That's what it was. Surely it can't be happening again.

But why has the Leo suddenly stopped firing?

He tells his TBS talker to hail her. The protocol of the escort group is that the ship making the attack will radio the assisting ship as to what station she should take, but *Leopold* has not radioed *Joyce*.

Wilcox drops the binoculars from his face and gives his TBS talker a stern glance as if to ask, "Is that damn radio of yours on, sailor?" But what he says is, "Keep trying the *Leopold*."

After several calls the talker gives his skipper a sheepish look. "Negative reply, sir."

Something's wrong. No artillery firing. No radio response. Where's the *Leopold*? Where is that goddamn sub?

He tells CIC to con the ship to a position of twenty-five hundred yards off the *Leopold*'s port beam, asks Bender if his boys on the sonar are having any more luck. Can they hear anything?

Not yet, says Bender.

Three weeks later at the board of inquiry, an officer on the board will ask Bender, "In view of the speeds of the *Joyce* and the leaks in the sound dome resulting in excess water noises, did you consider the sound searches carried on the night of 9-10 March effective?"

Bender will say, "The water noises on the port side were extremely high, but the condition started to develop about three days before and grew successively worse. This was apparently due to the fact that this lug had worked out of the bottom of the sound dome [like a wart on the bottom of the ship] as reported by a diver at Londonderry and also due to loose rivets on the port side of the dome. It was reported by the diver that three rivets were loose and probably would have vibrated at any speed. In addition to this, the diver reported the port side of the dome had been creased by some object striking it. Any of these conditions would have caused high water noise level. The three combined gave extremely high noise level at fifteen knots or over."

Wilcox is ruminating on Bender's difficulties with the sonar and still searching with his binoculars for the *Leopold* out there in the dark when he hears the TBS crackle. It almost makes him jump.

"Scotch, Scotch. This is Virgil. Come back, Scotch."

It's the talker on the *Poole*. His code name for his task group commander is Virgil. Virgil, Capt. Bill Kenner on the *Poole*, has clearly been listening to the *Joyce*'s repeated unanswered calls to the *Leopold*, code name Scotch. Kenner's getting worried, too, so he's making TBS calls of his own. He wants to know why in all hell the *Leopold*, Scotch, has not answered the *Joyce*, not answered Bourbon.

"CIC says *Leopold* has suddenly slowed to six knots, Skipper." Wilcox tenses with the news from his talker.

"Let's get the Aldis light going," the *Joyce*'s skipper tells his exec. He's asking for a signalman to start interrogating the *Leopold* with light signals in Morse code. One way or another he's going to find his sister ship, sonar or no sonar, radio or no radio. He's going to get to the bottom of Ken Phillips's sudden silence and the Leo's abrupt slowing from flank speed. The only question is can Wilcox do this without exposing himself to the enemy? What would his hero Adm. David Farragut do? Damn the torpedoes. Full speed ahead.

PART THREE

THINGS FALL APART

CHAPTER TWENTY

Goddamn

March 9, 1944, 2015 Hours

STANDING ON THE STARBOARD WING OF THE FLYING BRIDGE AT A PLACE known as the captain's pulpit, Wilcox still has his binoculars pressed to his face. During his years at sea, he has come to love his "second eyes," US Navy issue, Bureau of Ships, 7x50, Mark 28 binoculars by Bausch & Lomb. They bring clarity to the vague, the obscure, the mysterious. At the moment they are bringing a silhouette into focus against the silver glow of the moonshine on the sea. It's a ship wallowing in building seas three thousand yards off to starboard. The *Leopold*. But she doesn't look like the gallant man-of-war she was when he last saw her. She looks like a twisted, fractured bathtub toy or an angry child's drawing of a ship. DE 319 is bent, sway-backed. Her bow is canting off to starboard at an odd angle. The fantail is no longer a sleek trailing edge. It's pointed about 15 degrees above the horizon.

"She's showing a light, sir." A telephone talker is broadcasting the news from one of the sailors posted at the lookout station off the starboard side/rear of the flying bridge. The lookout station has four men in heavy foul weather jackets and blue knit watch caps pulled down over their faces. They have special chairs, each with a set of binoculars on a bracket along with a bearing dial and elevation indicator. A telephone talker at the lookout station communicates the location of contacts to the officer of the deck and CIC.

The OOD asks for a relative bearing.

"Midships, sir. Low down."

Wilcox squints into his Bausch & Lombs, thanks the Good Lord for young men with eyes like eagles. He can see it now that they have pointed it out. A dim light glows right at the waterline.

"Alter course, to starboard," he tells his talker and gives a new heading. Then he orders the engine room to slow to "all ahead one third."

He doesn't like going this slowly with at least one enemy sub around. At this speed he's an easy target for a U-boat, but if he approaches the *Leopold* any faster, he might overrun her. She appears dead in the water as the *Joyce* closes the distance between the two escorts to less than a mile.

"Any echoes from the submarine, Mr. Bender?" Wilcox keeps his voice flat, projects the sureness of a battle-seasoned veteran, a man in command of the situation.

"Negative, sir, but I think we are beginning to hear the *Leopold*." Bender says that the sound hut is picking up noises. Maybe a generator. A lot of strange squeaks and groans.

"Holy shit. Look at that." The voice of one of the starboard lookouts carries over the flying bridge before he catches himself. "Sorry, sir."

Wilcox doesn't respond to this breach of protocol because he, too, can see the damage to his sister ship. When he testifies before the board of inquiry next month, he will state, "A large hole was noticed in the port side of the other ship, extending from about frame fifty-eight to frame seventy-five, from waterline up through main deck into the deckhouse. *Leopold's* back was broken, and she was sagging badly, with port screw completely clear of the water as a trough of sea passes under her stern."

The wind is coming up, and as *Joyce* slows, she's starting to do what her crew calls the "tin can roll," 15 degrees port then starboard. The skipper and the other men on the flying bridge spread their legs and hold onto the steel rails of the bridge combing for balance. For several seconds no one says anything. It's as if none of them can believe what they are seeing, including Gerald Stern who is on the signal light.

"You see that, sir?" the OOD asks Wilcox.

"The light's moving around now," says the captain. "It's one of the battle lights or a flashlight. It's up on the first platform deck."

Wilcox may consider for a few seconds shining his big carbon arc light on the Leo to get a clearer look, but he decides against it. He has already made up his mind that she has been torpedoed. Why make himself or his sister ship even more obvious for Fritz to spot if he's out here in the dark somewhere watching this goddamn mess through his periscope? And what if there are two or more of Fritz? Don't the Germans sometimes use a decoy to draw escorts into a trap set by an entire pack of sea wolves?

He tells his talker to have CIC con the *Joyce* closer to the wreck.

The full moon is higher now and out of the clouds. At a distance of less than a half-mile from 319, the men on the *Joyce* can see shadows of men on the *Leopold* launching life rafts and floater nets.

"Light signals from the *Leopold*," says the lookouts' talker. "They see us."

Gerald Stern trains his eyes on an Aldis light flashing from the bow of 319. He doesn't have to think. Instantly, he's reading the Morse code. Short, long—A. Long, short, short, short—B. Short, long—A. Long, short—N. He knows the rest of the message even before the signaler finishes. Everyone on the flying bridge does. The Leo's men are signaling that they are abandoning ship.

Wilcox's response is instantaneous. He orders his ship to signal *Leopold* that *Joyce* is standing by. Then he takes the con back from CIC and orders a change of course. He aims to circle 319 to assess her situation. The skipper also calls for a change in speed, orders standard speed, fifteen knots. If Fritz is out there in the dark trying to get a bearing and speed on the *Joyce*, Wilcox is not going to make it easy.

"Advise Virgil [Kenner on the *Poole*] of the *Leopold*'s situation," he tells his TBS talker. "Request assistance."

Joyce starts a slow clockwise circle around the wreck. Now the men on the bridge can see figures on the bow dropping into the water.

"Those poor bastards," says someone.

"Amen," says someone else.

"Message coming in from Virgil, sir." It's the TBS talker.

"Yes?"

"He says use your best judgment. He can't spare us another escort."

Well, that's just goddamn perfect, isn't it? This is the kind of sentiment running through Wilcox's mind, the kind of thing that he will never say. He knows that Kenner has made the right decision. Virgil can't let his convoy transit Torpedo Junction with only three escorts. The Germans could have a field day. But this isn't a pretty picture. The convoy is already ten miles away and getting a mile farther every four minutes. These poor buggers from the *Leopold* are dropping into water that is at best 47 degrees. Fritz—and maybe his pals—are lurking down there somewhere close. And *Joyce* is on her own with shit for working radar and sonar. Situation normal—all fucked up.

Chapter Twenty-One

Over the Side

March 9, 1944, 2024 Hours

Sparky Nersasian and Luke Bobbitt can hear men yelling, "Abandon ship, abandon ship." The two gunners are still at the number two gun on the bow. Jerry Claus has eased his grip on Nersasian. Claus seems dead. He's sitting, propped against the ammo box with his good eye fixed on his groin. They leave him and climb over the edge of the gun deck and head down to their abandon-ship station, the number one life net.

Men are launching the life nets and life rafts. Immediately, some of them jump in the water. Bobbitt thinks they're crazy. They are leaping off the boat like they are taking a summer swim. The air reeks of spilling fuel oil.

You can't go over the side with all that clothing, thinks Bobbitt. He sits down and starts untying his shoes and taking off his heavy winter pants. But he's in no hurry. He knows the water is going to be freezing, and even though the bow has started to twist away from the stern of the ship, the bow still feels like it's going to float for a little while longer. The spooky thing is that it's starting to pitch up, to point to the sky, more and more as every minute passes.

One of the sailors is staring at the water and saying he can't swim when the captain, Ken Phillips, and the exec, Pete Cone, show up.

"Don't worry, men. You'll be picked up soon. God bless you all," says Phillips. Then he tells the kid who can't swim to get a life vest on.

Bobbitt realizes that he still doesn't have a life vest. The one he retrieved from the forecastle must have been the one Nersasian put on Claus. Meanwhile, more men have begun jumping off the ship into the life nets, big rubber balls bound together in an oval by rope and netting. The guys dropping into the life nets don't seem to be coming back up to the surface. They must be getting caught underwater in the netting. Nersasian thinks, *Holy shit. I'm not jumping in.*

A chief arrives on the scene and says that the men have to go into the water slowly otherwise the shock of the cold water could kill them. The chief rigs a line over the side and starts sending men down the line. Nersasian's contemplating going down the line, but Bobbitt still doesn't have a life vest. He's standing at the rail shaking hands with guys before they go over the side and start down the rope.

One guy says, "So long, Luke, I'll be seeing you."

"What the hell you worrying about? We'll be picked up in nothing flat. It's not our time yet." Bobbitt heads down the rope with no life vest.

Sparky Nersasian follows him, but he's not totally feeling Bobbitt's optimism. When Nersasian tells his niece Tory about this moment more than forty years later, he will say, "We're forty feet in the air. You can see the oil. There's bedlam. Guys are screaming. I go down the rope and this Polish kid is coming after me, a big son-of-a-gun. He's standing on my shoulders. His feet are on my shoulders. I yell, 'Ski, for the love of God, let me get down first, and I'll wait for you on the bottom.'

"The minute my feet touch the water, I say to myself, *This is it. No way am I getting out of this.* It's impossible. We're seven hundred miles from nowhere and there isn't a soul in sight, just guys screaming. Down I went, touched the water. He let go. He's sitting right on my shoulders and has me scissored with his feet. Down I go. He weighs two hundred pounds, and I'm trapped."

Bobbitt is already in the water. He pops up and looks around, sees the heads of other guys bobbing in the water near him. He never totally got his shoes off on deck. Now they feel heavy, and he bends underwater to take them off. A buddy grabs him and pulls him up.

"You giving up so soon?"

"Don't worry about me, Mac," Bobbitt says, "as soon as I get these shoes off, I'm leaving. I want to live awhile." He tugs off a shoe.

Nersasian doesn't know how he does it, but he gets free of his shipmate's scissor hold. When he pops to the surface the Polish kid is gone. The water is so cold it feels like thousands of little needles piercing his skin. He could give up right here, right now . . . except that Luke Bobbitt is calling his name.

———

While Bob Chandler is trying to calm the sailor with the head wound, another sailor throws him two life jackets and says, "You better abandon ship. Everybody else has already abandoned ship."

Chandler puts the life vest on the wounded guy who is still babbling incoherently, leads him out the starboard hatch and back aft. The wounded man is standing at the rail unable to move. Chandler goes to look for a life raft or net for them. He feels the ship quaking uneasily under him and knows that time is of the essence. He runs along the starboard side looking for rafts or nets in the water that have space for two more men.

When he spies one, he starts shouting to the men in it, asking if they have room for two more in the raft. Maybe they can't hear him because he gets no response. He climbs over the life lines, hangs on them so that the men in the raft can see him, hear him. He's midships, just about at the spot where the Leo is starting to tear herself in two. Sea water is starting to come aboard. He's still shouting, still getting no response. Just then the middle of the ship sags violently and a swell sweeps Chandler into the frigid water.

———

Not far from where Chandler has been sucked overboard, but on the other side of the ship, Warren Young is moving at a fast trot. He has just seen the torpedo smoking on the boat deck, and he's racing down the port ladder to get to his abandon-ship station, the number two life raft. He sees men starting to launch the life raft, wants to help, but someone says they need him in the galley. This is the area of the main deck right above the engine room where the torpedo struck, and the once-orderly galley is a shambles. There's a baker trapped underneath an immense range that has fallen on him, pinning his leg. The man's face grimaces with pain.

"Shoot me, please just shoot me," he says to Young.

But neither Young nor any of the other men have any intention of ending the man's life. They rally together and lift the stove off him while one of the guys pulls the baker clear. Someone buckles a life vest on him. Water has started to slosh over the galley floor. Everybody knows that at any moment this tin can could break in half . . . probably right at this very spot.

"You're going to be okay, buddy. We got to abandon ship now," says a good Samaritan.

The baker still lies on the floor, says that he can't move, doesn't want to drown. "Leave me a gun."

Young and others drag him to the number two life raft station. The raft is gone, but there's a scramble net hanging over the side for men to get into the water. This is obviously something the baker cannot negotiate.

"Just wait here," one of the guys tells him. "When the ship breaks, you'll just slide into the water and a raft will pick you up."

Wishful thinking. As far as Young can tell there are no rafts to be seen now. Still, raft or no raft, it's clearly time for him to go over the side. The ship's tearing steel sounds like the shrieks of an inconsolable baby. He needs to get away, get down this net and into the water. Thank God, at least, he's wearing a thick kapok life vest, not a flimsy blow-up one or dinky little life belt. The kapok vest might buy him some time to find his way to a raft.

⚓

After the order to abandon ship, Bill Miller follows the skipper, Pete Cone, and the rest of the men off the flying bridge. He goes down to the boat deck and helps one of the officers launch the number one life raft that hangs from the superstructure below the bridge on the starboard side. As soon as the raft launches, bunches of men jump for it. Miller goes in after it, but there are so many men clinging to it that he can't even get a handhold. The problem seems to be that the raft has landed upside down and men can't get into it. Remembering the film that he watched this afternoon about abandoning ship, Miller tries to swim away from the Leo so that he doesn't get sucked down when the ship sinks. But waves keep buffeting him against the hull. This is bad. He's going to die if he stays here. He thinks his best chance is to try to paddle around to the port side of the ship to escape the waves and find a raft or at least a life net with space.

Somehow he makes it. As he goes, he notices the huge, jagged hole in the port side midships. Water is flooding over the deck here as the ship continues to fold up on itself. Miller is feeling the cold of the water. It is really starting to slow him down, so he pulls himself back aboard the ship where the bending deck meets the water. At this point he could go aft to the fantail or forward to the bow. He spots men on the bow, the captain

Whaleboat on the USS *Slater* (same as on the *Leopold*). COURTESY DESTROYER ESCORT HISTORICAL MUSEUM, ALBANY, NEW YORK.

and some officers. This looks like good company so he heads forward to them. When he reaches the bow he finds Ken Phillips, Cone, and several other officers signaling 317 with an Aldis light. The officers are talking among themselves, and Cone tells Phillips that he believes that they still have time to gather the ship's top-secret papers and burn them.

Men are shouting for help from the water. Others are standing at the ship's rail trying to muster the courage to head down the rope after Bobbitt and Nersasian. Miller asks the captain why they don't lower the whaleboat off the boat deck. Phillips says something about how it can't be done, a davit has been smashed by the explosion. Miller's wondering what the hell the designers of this ship were thinking when they made it next to impossible to launch the big whaleboat in an emergency. Suddenly, the bow gives a big lurch and tilts steeply into the air. There's a guy caught in the port anchor, shouts someone. It's Chief Quartermaster Richard Leo Graham and he's dangling by one leg.

"Everybody in the water," orders the captain. "This thing is about to go."

Nobody needs to tell Miller a second time. As he follows some of the officers into the water, he catches a glimpse of the captain heading forward to the very bow of the ship. Phillips is checking to make sure everyone is off this end of the boat before he goes. A fella has to wonder if things are this bad back aft on the fantail?

CHAPTER TWENTY-TWO

What the Hell?

March 9, 1944, 2028 Hours

USS *JOYCE* IS STILL CIRCLING THE *LEOPOLD*. THE MOON DRIFTS IN AND out of the clouds. CIC has the con again. The ship is making fifteen knots, falling back to a range of three thousand yards from the wreck, when one of the *Joyce*'s two sonar men in the sound hut says that he has a contact. A weird one.

"It's coming toward us." The sonar man has his earphones pressed to his head with his hands.

John Bender, the sound officer, tells the sonar operator to put the noise on the speaker so that he can hear it too. Bender listens to the sound. He can hear the beat of a propeller.

"Bearing?"

"Two eight zero, sir."

"Distance?"

The sonar operator can't be sure. Definitely less than two thousand yards. He can't hear anything beyond that range, especially with the ship moving this fast and the leak in the sonar dome causing a distracting burbling noise that almost blots out any other sound. But whatever the range, the thing's aiming right for the *Joyce*'s port beam.

Bender concentrates on the sound, tries to separate it from the burbling noise caused by the leak. At the board of inquiry he will say, "The main thing that we noticed on the propeller noises was the lack of similarity of any torpedoes we heard before. I think both of my sound men and myself have heard the records [for training], and I have heard the German torpedoes before. This had a very different note. The noise was of a lower pitch, and it had none of the high whine, the screech of the torpedoes I have heard before. The noise seemed to be more of a water noise level than the previous torpedoes. There was no question that it was a torpedo. There was a definite propeller beat to it, but instead of a screech there was a much lower noise."

—— ·——

When Bender calls to Wilcox over the voice pipe from the sound hut, telling him that they've got what sounds like a torpedo heading for them, the skipper bends his ear to the tube to listen to the sound. To him it sounds like a train in a tunnel, maybe one of the obsolete air-driven torpedoes the Germans were using at the beginning of the war. It doesn't sound anything like the electrically driven T3 or T5 that the Ubootwaffe uses these days. Who the hell knows? But maybe the gods are on his side for the moment because just this afternoon he was rereading the protocol for dodging torpedoes.

"I have the con," he tells the OOD, then immediately orders the engines to go to emergency flank speed, rudder hard over to the right. He wants to turn away from the torpedo, put it on the stern. It might be coming at the *Joyce* at twice the current speed of the DE, but at least he can buy some time by running away from it, and he can make his ship the smallest possible target by showing only her thirty-foot fantail to the eel. This is the tactic that has been refreshed in his mind by his reading this afternoon.

The PA system warns the crew. There's an incoming torpedo. Brace for impact.

Suddenly, the men on the *Joyce* are thinking *Oh, shit, we're next.* No longer are 317's lookouts training their binoculars on 319. They are probing the shadowy seas for a torpedo wake amid the rising and breaking six-foot wind waves. But nobody is seeing anything. It's just Bender and his boys in the sound hut who are trying to keep a clear bearing on the strange noise beating toward them as their ship tries to maneuver out of danger.

Later, at the board of inquiry, men will say that the *Leopold* broke in half sometime between 2020 hours and 2040 hours. Nobody knows for sure. No one on the *Leopold* is checking his watch right now, and nobody on the *Joyce* is looking. If they were, they would see that at this very moment she has come apart, become two floating halves with the bow section rolling on its starboard side then going keel up.

Almost nobody on the *Joyce* is thinking any longer about all those guys jumping into the water off the *Leopold* . . . except Bob Wilcox. As he cons his ship into a steep right turn and the *Joyce* leans hard over to port from centrifugal force, he grabs the bullhorn that they keep on the bridge and points it toward the fractured halves of his sister ship.

"We are dodging torpedoes. God bless you. We will be back." His heart is pounding with adrenaline . . . and probably starting to ache from what he fears is yet to come tonight.

Shouts rise up from the fantail. "Torpedo."

The chief radioman turns to the chief gunner's mate and points to something, maybe a torpedo's bubbling wake, crossing the *Joyce*'s stern.

Wilcox must hear David Farragut's voice in his head again. Damn the torpedoes. . . .

CHAPTER TWENTY-THREE

Hold Your Breath

March 9, 1944, 2030 Hours

PING. THE SOUND ECHOES THROUGH U-255. YOU DON'T HAVE TO BE THE Funker wearing earphones to hear it. Ping. Unconsciously, men hold their breath. Ping. Dieter Hengen, the first watch officer, has probably started swearing in his head, started composing the narrative that he will one day write about tonight for Horst Bredow, the long-term curator of the Deutsches U-boot Museum in Cuxhaven. Ping. He's young and anxious with dreams of love and life after this war. Ping. A less battle weary skipper than Erich Harms might think, *Here we go.* Ping. He might feel the thrill of the fox and hounds game beginning in earnest, might feel that his chance is coming to prove to himself, his crew, and Grand Admiral Dönitz that he can outsmart the American hounds. Ping. Every seven seconds, ping.

But this pinging is something that Harms has heard all too many times from English and Americans hunting his U-boat. The source of that ping is the echo location device that the English call "asdic," a term with its origins in the Anti-Submarine Division of the Royal Navy, and the Americans call "sonar," an acronym for SOund Navigation And Ranging. These pings are the sound of the second Feger that he knew would be coming for him. Ping is not just the probing of his enemy's sonar. Ping is the sound of fear.

Who knows what kind of death and destruction Harms's T5 has wrought on the first destroyer? Perhaps just a wound, but possibly total devastation. Unless he surfaces to see, a submariner will never truly know the effects of a torpedo launched blindly during a crash dive. One thing is certain. The T5 hit its mark and one American destroyer escort is in pain. The Funker can still hear it on 255's hydrophones. The wounded American's sister is surely hungry for German blood now, Harms's blood. He's at 160 meters, nearing 255's maximum service depth. But maybe he should push the boat deeper because these pings sound clear as a bell, the heavy whir of the enemy's props rumble through 255 like there's no shield of thermocline overhead to deflect sounds. If he doesn't do something fast, the second destroyer will find him. Then the chances are just about nil that he will ever breathe fresh air or see home again.

Over his five years in the Kriegsmarine, Harms has committed the U-boat Commanders Handbook, known as the "U.Kdt.Hdb," to memory. He has lived by its fundamental premise:

The theoretical knowledge of the weapon, and of the appropriate tactics, must be supplemented, in the last resort, by the decisive requirement of a war-like spirit and an audacious outlook. The essence of submarine warfare is the offensive! For the commander of a submarine, therefore, the maxim: "He who wants to be victorious on the sea must always attack!" has special meaning.

How many times has he heard his leaders promote a ruthless and indefatigable spirit with phrases like "The weaknesses of the submarine must be offset by clever tactics, unscrupulous use, and obstinate persistence even when the chances of success appear slender"?

And yet, at times like this, with men dying from his torpedo in the waves overhead and a four-out-of-five chance that he and his crew will soon be bones lost in an iron coffin, not the glorious Nordic souls of warriors on their way to Valhalla, a man, a real leader who has seen the hell of war too long, may wonder. He may fret deep down in his core where no one can see. He may ponder whether words like "war-like spirit and an audacious outlook" or "unscrupulous use" have any place in a manual on leadership . . . or whether they are patriotic propaganda and gobbledygook written by someone too old or too privileged to serve aboard a *Frontboot* running for its life in the cold North Atlantic.

But this moment with the pings of a Feger ringing through 255 every seven seconds is no time to get lost in misgivings. It is a moment to try to save his ship and his crew. The "U.Kdt.Hdb" is not without merit when it comes to offering up tactics for a situation like this.

If the submarine is forced to dive after the underwater attack, on account of the dangerous proximity of enemy hunting units, then it should first go down at full speed in a direction leading away from the scene of action and the direction of the torpedo . . .

Harms checks off in his mind each bit of advice he follows from the handbook. *Richtig.* Right. Doing that. Diving fast, turning away from the torpedo track, running.

After the boat has dived, and the steering gear has been adapted to the required depth, put everything out of action, listen carefully, in order to find out what the enemy is doing, and act accordingly . . .

Richtig.

Do not go down to an unnecessary depth, as this may also be dangerous: the stern stuffing boxes and other fastenings leak badly, the joints are subject to heavy strain. Always choose the lesser danger, by weighing up the danger from depth charges against the danger of an increased [pressure] eruption of water.

Richtig.

Eliminate all sources of noise in the submarine: stop all auxiliary machinery which is not indispensable (pumps, ventilators, compressors, periscope motor, gyroscopic compass—above all, the secondary gyroscopes—etc.); main rudder and hydroplane should be operated by hand; pumping out, and trimming, with air; depth steering as far as possible only by head list, and then trimming by hand.

Richtig.

Maintain absolute silence of the crew on board the submarine; speaking in low tones, working silently, moving about in stocking feet, etc.

Richtig.

Go down very deep; the deeper the position of the submarine, the greater the probability of being incorrectly sound-located.

The Old Man is mulling over the mixed messages that the handbook gives about the wisdom of going deep when a shock, a jolt rattles the dishes in the pantry and rocks U-255. A muffled rumble rolls through the boat. Lights flicker. Men who are not holding onto things in the Zentrale drop to their knees or find themselves thrown against pipes, valves, and bulkheads. Some are already bleeding.

A second shock hits.

Blechedosen, says someone. Tin cans. Wabos. These two are not very close. But still . . .

The "U.Kdt.Hdb" offers Harms unsettling counsel.

If attacked with depth charges, keep a close watch on all joints, as these easily become loose as a result of vibrations, making possible large eruptions of water.

Was nun? What now?

CHAPTER TWENTY-FOUR

Hunting

March 9, 1944, 2036 Hours

"CAN YOU STILL HEAR THAT THING, MR. BENDER?" WILCOX MEANS THE supposed torpedo that he put on his stern when he left the men on the *Leopold* abandoning ship.

The ASW officer says, "Negative." He and his crew in the sound hut of the *Joyce* can't hear anything but water noise. The ship is still steaming at emergency flank speed, about twenty-three knots, and rumbling with the vibration of her diesels running at full bore. The sound of rushing water over the sonar dome has blanked out all reception. Bender tells his skipper that the leak in the sonar dome seems to have gotten worse. Maybe if they slow the boat down, the sound men might hear something besides water noise.

DEs like the *Joyce* depend on their sonar for detecting U-boats underwater. Known as the QGB, the DE's sonar unit keeps company with a tactical range recorder and an attack plotter in the sound hut forward of the flying bridge. Sonar works by sending a sound wave through the water, in this case a metallic pinging. When that sound wave hits something solid like a submerged U-boat, it causes an echo. The sonar operator, or the machine itself, uses the time the echo takes to return to calculate the distance to a target. On the *Joyce* the sonar gear functions like a beam of light. It emanates from the sonar dome mounted underwater near the ship's bow and scans a small area at a time. The ship's crew must shift the sonar dome by hand to scan broadly around the ship and to lock in the bearing of the target.

Because of the interference from the water noise, Wilcox knows that the soundmen on the *Joyce* have the signal strength, the "gain," cranked way down on the sonar to tune out the water noise. But even with the gain turned down low, the sub out there must be able to hear the pinging a mile away. Not a good thing. If the German gets a decent sound bearing on the *Joyce*, he's in a good position to set up for another shot. This is the kind of thing that Wilcox worries about. But not the only thing.

His sound men have heard a couple of explosions as *Joyce* has been running for her life. The explosions sounded like depth charges going off. Goddamn. The crew of the Leo must not have set some of her depth charges on "safe" after the torpedoing. Now the Mark 9 depth charges are spilling into the sea and detonating as 319 breaks up. She's probably killing her own men who are in the water. What the hell else is ready to blow on her? There is a lot of ordnance on a DE. *Joyce* has to get back to those men before it's too late.

Wilcox checks his watch. It has been eight minutes since he turned away from the torpedo. Surely, it has passed him by now. He damn well wishes Bender could confirm that the *Joyce* is in the clear. But with the echo of the strange-sounding torpedo no longer heard by the sound men, he's just going to have to take his chances. He wants that sub. It can't be far from here, and maybe the bastard is lurking at periscope depth, preparing for another shot at him. Maybe it's just waiting for him to stop and try to rescue *Leopold* survivors and then whack him, too.

"Hard right rudder," orders the skipper. He tells his quartermaster to steer the reciprocal course of the alleged torpedo, hold the *Joyce* on 280 degrees. He aims to track that torpedo to its source. "Let's get this son of a bitch," he says. But what he must be thinking is *Let's get the U-boat before he gets us. Let's get him so we can start picking two hundred good men out of this frigid water.*

―◆―

Once *Joyce* is pointed back in the direction that the strange-sounding torpedo came from, Wilcox slows the ship to twenty-one knots, flank speed, and asks Bender if he can hear anything on the QGB yet.

Only water noise, reports the ASW officer. At the board of inquiry, Bender will say, "The search could be conducted to starboard and on the port side to about 315 [degrees] relative. Beyond that bearing the water noise was too high to search there. To hear our outgoing transmission [a ping] at all, we had to turn down our receiver sensitivity, which naturally would limit the range of receiving echoes. Cruising the next morning in this area at fifteen knots, we were getting ranges ahead about three thousand yards on the remaining portion of the *Leopold*. This, however, was a very large target and picked up ahead. I don't feel that echoes could have been received at this range on the port beam."

Staring into the darkness ahead through his Bausch & Lombs, the skipper can see nothing except the flash of silvery waves when the moon breaks free of the clouds. He can tell that the wind is coming up and the seas are building. If and when he ever gets to the Leo's men, fetching them out of the seas in these conditions will be no picnic. But right now he can't even see the *Leopold*. She must be somewhere up ahead at maybe two or three miles, but where?

He asks CIC if they still have 319 on the radar. It's a stupid question. He knows that the radar is barely functional. It can't see shit beyond a couple thousand yards, but, damn it, he's still hoping when he hears the lookouts' talker pipe up. The wreck of the *Leopold* is about 30 degrees off the port bow at about two miles.

Everybody on the flying bridge trains his binoculars in the direction of the wreck. She's clearly silhouetted by the moonlight now. *Leopold* is broken in two. There seems to be the glow of lights on the stern. No doubt everyone on the bridge is thinking that there but for the grace of God goes the *Joyce*. No doubt, everyone is thinking about all those men in the water. They know that the life rafts can't even hold a quarter of the Leo's crew. They saw that the whaleboat had not been launched. Obviously there are a lot of men in 47-degree water praying for a quick rescue.

No one more than Wilcox wants to help those men. He joined the Coast Guard to save lives, not fight a war. But he can't risk his ship by stopping for men in the water with a U-boat out here possibly preparing a second attack.

He bends to the voice pipe, "Damn it, Mr. Bender, find me that sub." *Joyce* doesn't have all the time in the world.

CHAPTER TWENTY-FIVE

Broken

March 9, 1944, 2020–2040 Hours

Sparky Nersasian and Luke Bobbitt feel trapped by the *Leopold*'s bow. Along with a dozen other sailors, they are holding onto a floater net. Some men seem frozen with panic as the waves pin the net and the men holding onto it against the steel plates of the bow. Bobbitt is shouting at Nersasian and the others to push the net away from the hull. He's pushing against the hull like a madman, but the waves are still pinning the men and the net here. Nersasian can see that Bobbitt's hands are already swollen to the size of mittens from the effort and the cold.

"We've got to get away from the ship. It's going under," Nersasian tells Bobbitt. He's a strong swimmer after twenty-one summers at the beach back in Salem, Massachusetts, and he feels like he's swimming at ninety-eight miles per hour, beating the water with his hands and his feet. But he's only moving about three or four feet a minute.

Bobbitt is at his side. He knows that Nersasian is right to leave the net and these fear-frozen men. *I'm getting out of here*, thinks Bobbitt, *I don't know where but I'm going. You don't want to be around a ship that's sinking. Maybe she'll blow up. Maybe she'll catch another torpedo. Maybe she'll sink and suck you down with her when she goes.* He doesn't have a life vest but the arms of his jungle jacket have trapped air. They are keeping him afloat like a child's water wings.

After a few minutes of desperate swimming, Bobbitt and Nersasian pause and look back. The bow is starting to roll over. Guys are leaping off. Some are still on the tilting deck praying to God and too afraid to move. Men have begun to scream for their mothers. Nersasian and Bobbitt swim like hell into the darkness. Neither of them has any sense of how long this goes on, the labored stroking with their arms, the kicking. When Nersasian finally stops to catch his breath, he looks over and sees that Bobbitt has what looks like a wooden cross in his right hand.

"It floated," he says. "I just picked it up."

Decades later Nersasian will tell his niece Tory, "It looked like it was made. Like something you would wear, [like] it was bought in a store. A piece of wood from furniture or the galley. Don't have any idea where it came from. All of a sudden, and out of nowhere, for no reason at all, there's a raft."

After spotting the *Leopold*'s loose torpedoes and finding the raft at his abandon-ship station gone, Glyone Mahaffy goes back over to the port side of the bow and joins men climbing down a scramble net into the water as the ship breaks in half. There's no raft, no life net, no nothing. Only dark ocean. Men are trying to swim away from the ship, fearing that it will suck them down as it sinks. But they can't get away. The wind seems to be blowing the ship right onto the men. And Mahaffy's got another problem. His inflatable life belt keeps throwing him face-down in the water every time he stops to rest. As the Coast Guard and Navy will learn after far too many drownings, Mahaffy's problem with his life belt is all too common. Many died of drowning during the D-Day invasion by wearing the life belt around their waist rather than under the armpits, thereby forcing their faces into the water.

He thinks, *To hell with this.* He's going to drown if he stays in the water with this life belt on, so he swims back to the ship where it has broken in two and pulls himself aboard the stern section. He lies there on the flooding deck until he feels the circulation return to his legs and he can stand. Then he heads back aft toward the K-gun launchers. Looking over the side he sees a raft with only two men in it. It's like the raft appeared out of nowhere, but he's not one to ask metaphysical questions at a moment like this. He jumps for it and hopes for the best.

Bill Miller is drifting back along the port side of the Leo to the very stern when the ship breaks up. He has been pushing himself away from the hull with outstretched legs. Suddenly, the stern rises high out of the water and the suction draws him right underneath the fantail, but now it's coming down on top of him. He covers his head with his hands, feels himself getting driven down into the frigid water. Then a rush of water squirts him out the other side of the fantail. He looks up and sees some men up there. One's actually straddling the stern running light like it's a saddle. Someone shouts down asking him how the water is. At another moment he might well have shouted back up for the man to go fuck himself, but right now he can't be bothered because he spots something out ahead. Not much more than a shadow. But squinting, Miller sees it's a life raft, about fifty feet away. And it has only about five guys in it.

He can barely swim in all his winter gear. But a current lifts him up and carries him along. In just two or three strokes he's at the raft and men are helping him aboard. It's almost like he's been washed right into Paradise. One of the angels is Glyone Mahaffy.

Richard Forrester knows that the Leo has split apart as he double-times it back aft to the fantail. It feels like he's walking on one of those shifting floors in a fun house, but it sounds like the end of the world. He knows that the ship has ripped in two right at the spot where he saw the loose Mark 15 torpedo resting on the 20mm ready ammo box. He sees the torpedo officer Ensign Tillman gather a group of several dozen men on the fantail. Maybe someone should tell Tillman about the loose "fish"; maybe there is some way to disarm the torpedoes before the shit hits the fan.

But if Forrester was ever going to tell Tillman about the torpedo problem, his moment is lost when the deck gives an immense lurch beneath him.

Gale Fuller is on the fantail, too. He sees the Leo's signal mast wobble. Then it appears to begin to fall to starboard. But it's not just the mast, a

Fantail on the USS *Slater* (same as on the *Leopold* where crew was awaiting rescue). COURTESY DESTROYER ESCORT HISTORICAL MUSEUM, ALBANY, NEW YORK.

spectral shadow in the moonshine, that is falling. The entire bow of the ship has separated from the stern and is rolling over. To some of the men watching, it appears that the bridge superstructure breaks loose from the hull as the bow rolls. The funnel sinks into the sea. Antiaircraft cannons seem to tumble after it. Nobody knows what has happened to the torpedo launcher or the loose torpedoes.

The forward deck of the fantail is now slipping beneath choppy seas. The entire stern half of the ship is starting to cant upward. Three or four men are scrambling up on its ragged port side edge near the machine shop hatch. They are officers, and they are calling for help. They are saying the skipper needs help. A chief motor machinist shouts to Forrester and Fuller to come to the rescue. They see that one officer named Evans is bleeding from a gash in his forehead. Another soaking wet officer has an arm around the waist of the skipper Ken Phillips and is holding him up, trying to help him walk. Phillips has a head wound and an injured leg. He looks dazed and out of breath. Apparently, he and the other officers got thrown from the ship when the bow rolled and the superstructure toppled. Fuller and Forrester take one officer's arms, wrap them around their shoulders, and help him back to the fantail. Other sailors are aiding the captain. They lay him down on a depth charge rack. Who's in charge now?

Chapter Twenty-Six

On Our Own

March 9, 1944, 2045 Hours

STAY AFLOAT. KEEP MOVING. STAY WARM. THESE ARE THE THOUGHTS GOING through Sparky Nersasian's mind as he strokes toward the empty raft. *And spit that shit out.* The surface of the water is slick with fuel oil spilling from the sinking *Leopold.* The oil tries to flood his mouth every time he breathes. It clots in his throat, his nose. Tastes like the cough medicine his mother used to feed him as a kid. Burns too. His eyes hurt like hell from being bathed in oil, but the kid who stood up to Jack Dempsey's thugs in the ring at Manhattan Beach is not going down without a fight. He digs deep into himself for inspiration, finds Puccini's aria "Nessun Dorma" as he often does. Here in the dark it seems to speak to him with peculiar relevance as the words proclaim that nobody will sleep tonight while the stars tremble with love and hope. What really energizes him, what drives him forward toward the raft, is the climax of the aria:

Dilegua, o notte!	*Vanish, o night!*
Tramontate, stelle!	*Fade, you stars!*
Tramontate, stelle!	*Fade, you stars!*
All'alba vincerò!	*At dawn, I will win!*
Vincerò! Vincerò!	*I will win! I will win!*

He's belting the lyrics out in his head as he throws an arm over the side of the raft and clings to it. *Vincerò!* Victory.

The raft is constructed of balsa wood and covered with canvas. It's as if he has crawled aboard a giant doughnut with wooden grating in its hole. It is floating upside down, but he doesn't care. He already knows that he is one of the lucky ones. The keen analytical mind that in future years will earn Sparky Nersasian a membership to MENSA as a certified genius has long ago done the math. DEs like the *Leopold* and her sisters only carry four so-called "twenty-five-man life rafts" for a crew of two hundred souls. And the truth is that these rafts can only carry about twelve men sitting on the sides. The rest of the men must remain in the water and hang on ropes strapped around the edge of the raft. Nersasian finds it beyond ironic that the Coast Guard that makes and enforces regulations for lifesaving apparatus on ships outfits a destroyer escort with only enough rafts to get fewer than a third of the crew out of the water. Even if the Leo's whaleboat, which can carry about thirty men, could be launched, more than half of his shipmates would have no way to escape this cold-ass water. The floater nets have already shown themselves to be lethal substitutes for rafts.

Why is it that the *Leopold* carries the absolute legal minimum number of rafts required of a ship her size? Why do the freighters and tankers in the convoy, with crews of less than half the number of the *Leopold*'s, carry as many rafts as the DE and carry more lifeboats? When this subject has come up during bull sessions on the mess deck or in the berthing quarters, the men always reach the same unsettling conclusion. Someone says, "Face facts, Mack. We are expendable."

Well not me. Not tonight, thinks Nersasian. *Vincerò!*

❦

Luke Babbitt is foaming at the mouth. He hopes it's from the oil on the water, not a symptom that his life is running out of him as he swims toward the raft. His legs are cramping. His chest hurts. His heart hurts. The sea feels alternately like a solid mass of steel around him holding him back from the raft, then like knives hacking into his arms and legs. He has begun to puke after every few strokes. But he's hugging the wooden cross that he found, and it is keeping him afloat.

He can tell that he's starting to lose it because he can't keep his mind focused on reaching the raft. His thoughts keep drifting off. He remembers winning a contest as a kid to see who could swim in really cold water the longest. He recalls sled-riding on a frozen lake and breaking through the ice. He couldn't pull himself back onto the ice without the help of a friend.

Then he's thinking about his last liberty in New York with his friend Big John Augsten. They had played high school football together, joined the coasties together, shipped out on the Leo together. It had been really cold that night of liberty in the city. Bobbitt and Augsten had dashed from beer joint to beer joint for slugs of booze, but they couldn't get warm. Augsten suggested that it would be nice to have a quart or two of hooch on the life raft to warm you up. Bobbitt thought it was a damn fool idea back then, but Sparky Nersasian and some other guys added a massive number of raisins to a water keg attached to one of the Leo's life rafts in hopes that the raisins would ferment and turn the water to homebrew. Maybe this is the raft. He sure hopes so because he can't last much longer in this frigid water. He needs something to warm him up. His shipmates' voices are pleading in the dark, echoing over the water. "Please help me. I'm drowning." One of those poor bastards could be Johnny Augsten. One could soon be Bobbitt.

When he reaches the raft a dozen or more men have pulled themselves aboard. The raft is so packed that it is nearly submerged by the weight of the men. There's no more room on the raft. Guys are clinging to the sides. He knows some of them—Sparky and Harry Daube. Bobbitt's afraid to let go of the wooden cross that's kept him afloat. Maybe he'll just stay here in the water. He's feeling warm and sleepy when a voice in the back of his head starts screaming at him, "You're quitting and it's not your time." He tells a chief yeoman who is sitting on the edge of the raft to beat him in the face. "Hit me with everything you got." Only pain can keep him awake. He knows that if he goes to sleep, it will be forever.

⚓

Bill Miller, Glyone Mahaffy, Warren Young, and a half-dozen others have made it aboard the number four life raft. It has been drifting along the port side of the Leo's fantail. Like Nersasian, Bobbitt, and Daube's raft, this one is upside down, too. The men have been debating whether to get off the raft and try to flip it so that they can get the paddles and supplies secured in the bottom of the raft, but the majority say they don't want to get back in the cold-ass water.

"We got to get away from the ship," says one of the men. Everyone knows what he means. In the abandoning ship training film that they watched this afternoon, the message was loud and clear. You have to make getting away from a sinking ship your first priority. Otherwise, it will suck you down.

But getting sucked down is not the immediate problem. The wind is pinning the raft against the ship, and little by little the raft has been drifting back to the very stern of the fantail. With each swell the stern is rising farther above the waves. Bill Miller can see the ship's screws rising and falling like immense guillotine blades preparing to crash down on the raft. Mahaffy has found a board and is using it as a paddle. Other men are frantically scooping at the water with their arms. Everyone is trying to steer the raft away from the rising and falling stern. But it's not possible, and the next time the stern slams down in a swell, it lands on the raft, driving it under water. When the raft squirts out the other side of the ship, several men are missing. Most are in the water.

—◆—

Mahaffy, Miller, and Young climb back aboard. They are shaking from the cold water. The moon has ducked back behind some clouds. The night is an opaque, dark gray. The *Joyce* is nowhere in sight. The raft has finally drifted away from the *Leopold*'s fantail.

"Looks like we're on our own now," says someone.

Chapter Twenty-Seven

Making the Best

March 9, 1944, 2100 Hours

GALE FULLER IS SITTING ON THE FANTAIL DECK, LEANING AGAINST A depth charge rack and wondering if these suckers are going to blow.

He knows that at least one or two already have, not more than ten or fifteen minutes ago, even though Mark 9 depth charges were supposed to be set on safe. Fuller had helped a crew of men disarm the depth charges. But then someone had the bright idea that the fantail might stay afloat longer if they jettisoned the Mark 9s to reduce weight. Within thirty or forty seconds of pitching the first depth charge overboard, the damn thing went off. There was no geyser of water, but the whole fantail shook. The Mark 9 must have been very deep when it detonated. But, still, the concussion had to have been hell on those guys in the water. A second charge that slipped overboard might have gone off too. What in the name of God Almighty is going to happen if the fantail goes down and dumps its load of more than one hundred depth charges into the sea? Is the Leo going to blow all her boys to smithereens?

"No more tossing depth charges," skipper Ken Phillips says.

His voice is weak as he lies on a depth charge rack with his eyes closed, soaking wet and trembling. Quite a few of the men here on the fantail are wet and cold. Some like Fuller got soaked by the seas thrown up when the torpedo exploded under the ship. Others like the captain, Lt. (jg) Arthur B. Evans, and seaman Bob Chandler have climbed back aboard after being in the water.

Fuller hears Ens. William Noel Tillman telling the captain to rest easy, telling the men around him to take heart. The *Joyce* will be back. Rescue will come. He eyes the nasty gash in the forehead of his fellow officer Art Evans, sees the blood pasted over Evans's face, but doesn't flinch.

This is what we're going to do, Tillman tells the dozens of men gathering at the stern. First, he's going below through the aft steering compartment and into the crews' quarters. An emergency generator has kicked on. There are functioning lights below deck, but who knows for how long? He says he's going to find first aid kits, blankets, and food. He'll be back in three shakes of a lamb's tail.

There's a note of confidence and assurance in Tillman's voice that seems to soften the pounding of Fuller's heart. He knows that he's witnessing one of those moments when heroes are born. Tillman's taking command of the situation. He's only twenty-three years old, but he's mature for his age. He's already married, with his wife Mary Seldan Tillman back at 5616 West Madison Street in Chicago. But at the moment, he's not thinking about Mary. He's thinking about his shipmates and mustering the can-do spirit for which tin can sailors are becoming famous. Tonight his poise, presence of mind, and valor will earn him a Bronze Star for meritorious service in a combat zone as well as a Purple Heart. The citation on the USCG Roll of Valor will read:

TILLMAN, William N.
ENS, USCG
Bronze Star (deceased)
For heroic service while serving as assistant gunnery and torpedo officer aboard the USS LEOPOLD during the sinking of that vessel in the Atlantic on March 9, 1944. Unmindful of his own danger, ENS Tillman courageously remained in the after section of the ship following the attack and working desperately to effect all possible safety measures, continued his valiant efforts until the LEOPOLD went down. His inspiring devotion to duty in the face of grave peril was in keeping with the highest traditions of the service.

Within ten minutes Tillman is back on deck passing out blankets, sweaters, chocolate bars, cigarettes, a bottle of whiskey, emergency lights, antiseptic cleansers, and bandages. He also has one big light from the repair locker to signal the *Joyce*.

"All hands count off," he says.

It's a clear order, and the men follow. When the tally is complete, thirty-six men have chimed in. Tillman, Capt. Ken Phillips, the wounded Lt. (jg) Art Evans, Lt. Robert Wescott, and Ens. Charles W. Valaer are the *Leo's* officers on the stern. Torpedoman Richard Forrester and Electrician's Mate Jeremiah Bowen are here too.

Tillman tells the men that the fantail is flooding. Watertight doors and bulkheads have been breached. The key is to try to keep afloat until the *Joyce* comes back to rescue them. Everybody needs to put on the best life vest available, one made of kapok if possible, and go as far aft as possible to the most buoyant part of the wreck. The men move. Some hang off the taffrail. Richard Forrester is straddling the stern light like it's a horse. Men pass the cigarettes to their buddies, break off pieces of chocolate bar for themselves, then pass the candy to the guy next to them. The whiskey's making the rounds too. It tastes like Liberty and New York and careless youth.

"Who knows a good joke?" asks Tillman.

Seventy years later Gale Fuller will no longer remember the jokes told tonight, but here's one that has been making the rounds among the coasties and Navy men. It's a joke that has resurfaced in the Navy and Coast Guard over generations in one form or another.

It's a dark and foggy night off the east coast of Ireland. A Royal Navy ship receives an incoming transmission with an Irish lilt. "Please alter your course 20 degrees to the south to avoid a collision."'

Royal Navy ship. "This is His Majesty's man-of-war. Alter your course."

Irish voice. "Negative. Alter your course to avoid a collision."'

Royal Navy ship. "*If you do not alter your course 20 degrees north, you will feel the mighty wrath of the King's navy.*"

Irish voice. "*I say again, you must alter your course 20 degrees south to avoid a collision.*"

Royal Navy ship. "*This is the HMS King George V, we are the crown jewel of the Royal Navy with the firepower of a full armored division. We will not alter our course.*"

Irish voice. "*This is a lighthouse. Your option.*"

Hoots are rising from the gathering of men on the fantail as the jokes flow. Someone says, "Pass the bottle." A seaman offers up a Coast Guard joke. It may well be this riddle:

"What are the five most dangerous things you're going to hear in the coast guard?"

One. A seaman saying, "I learned this in Boot Camp . . ."

Two. A petty officer urging, "Trust me, Sir . . ."

Three. A lieutenant (jg) proclaiming, "Based on my experience . . ."

Four. A lieutenant announcing, "I was just thinking . . ."

Five. A master chief gunner's mate chuckling, "Watch this shit . . ."

Even Ken Phillips is laughing now. Fuller's thinking that if his shipmates can keep the jokes coming, maybe these tin can sailors will have the stuff to survive until the *Joyce* comes back. But then the fantail gives a shudder. The stern lurches higher out of the water, and another twelve feet of deck at the forward end of the wreck slips beneath the sea. The lights below flicker.

PART FOUR

THE DARKEST HOURS

CHAPTER TWENTY-EIGHT

Life and Death

March 9, 1944, 2115 Hours

MILLER, MAHAFFY, AND YOUNG ARE STARTING TO WORRY ABOUT THEIR shipmates in life raft number four, a lot. Lt (jg) William E. Spencer, the supply officer, is aboard their up-side-down raft. The lieutenant is lying deep in the water on the grating in the raft. He's mumbling about thirty-five thousand dollars in cash left in the ship's safe. Over and over again he keeps telling the guys on his raft that they have to get back to the ship. He needs to get that money. All that money. It's his responsibility. Then he goes silent. He's still wearing his officer's cap. His eyes are open. His mouth is open. Mahaffy is sitting on the edge of the raft, and Spencer's leaning against his legs. Now Mahaffy's afraid to look at Spencer.

A seaman named Seymour Bressler is beside Spencer not doing much better. He's in the water up to his shoulders. He keeps asking where the ship is. He says the *Joyce* is going to pick them up. He's sure of it. But it better hurry. It really better hurry.

One of the other guys says that the *Joyce* has gone off. It was under attack by torpedoes. But Bressler keeps asking where the *Joyce* is. His questions grow more insistent. Now he's bleeding freely from the nose and mouth. His shipmates try to lift him out of the water, but he flails at them with his arms and legs. He tumbles over and over in the water at the center of the raft. Then his mouth sags open and he lies still.

Nobody says the obvious. The poor guy's dead. He's gone. And so is Spencer.

"I stuck my arm through a ring in the raft and started to pick up guys," Sparky Nersasian will tell his niece Tory more than forty years after the event. "The raft safely, comfortably holds ten or twelve people. I'm hanging in the water and the next think I know twenty to twenty-five men are on the raft. No way could I get on there. Geeze. I was tired. Think I'll take a nap. Off I go. Bang! Luke [Bobbitt] punches me in the nose. 'Stay awake.'"

On the night of March 9, 1944, Nersasian's learning firsthand how fast 46-degree water can disable and kill. He has seen all those guys jump into the floater net off the bow and never come up. After their plunge into cold water, receptors in their skin triggered an array of physiological responses. The first was a gasp reflex. If this happens when a man is underwater and he inhales, he's on his way to drowning.

If he is lucky enough to not draw water into his lungs, he has other issues. His heart rate and blood pressure will spike. He will begin to hyperventilate. At this point he may panic, amplifying his cardio-pulmonary problems. These events can stop his heart. But even if his heart keeps beating, without a flotation device that cradles his head and face above the water, he will have difficulty breathing while experiencing the shock of cold water.

Cold shock peaks during the first minute of immersion. If a seaman in this water is still alive and conscious after a minute, his body will begin to shiver to keep itself warm. But it is fighting a losing battle. Water cools a human body twenty-five times faster than air. Within a few minutes, the muscles of a body's limbs will grow dysfunctional. Bodily fluids will start to congeal in the tissue. This is what Sparky Nersasian is feeling. First, he lost sensation in his fingers, hands, toes, and feet. Now his legs and arms are beginning to go numb.

He has all but lost his ability to grasp things or even move his limbs. Trying to swim during the early stages of cold shock and hypothermia have only hastened his body's loss of heat and accelerated the paralysis of his limbs. As the core temperature drops below 95 degrees Fahrenheit in a human body, a person often becomes disoriented. He may hallucinate.

He will feel very sleepy. Eventually he will become unconscious. Then he will die. Nersasian needs to get out of this water or he will be literally or functionally dead in minutes.

Like Bill Spencer and Seymour Bressler in raft number four, men are dying in Nersasian's raft too. As they die, their shipmates slide the bodies over the side to make room for the living like Nersasian and Bobbitt, who are hanging onto the outside of the raft. It's a grim business jettisoning the bodies. There is almost no talking on the raft except to say, "The poor bastard's gone. Help me get him over."

The men wearing the fewest clothes are dying first. One reason that Nersasian and Bobbitt are still alive is because they dressed in four layers of clothing for the freezing conditions of manning the ready gun. In this water all those layers are slowing their loss of body heat.

"I finally get on the raft," Nersasian will tell his niece. "There's this carpenter's mate Walter, lying in my lap. Luke says, 'Hit him, hit him hard. Don't let him go to sleep.'"

Nersasian hits Ward. Hits him again but there's no response. He tries to reach down and lift Ward out of the water, but it is impossible. The raft is crammed with so many men.

Nersasian has no room to move. "I look down at my legs and they are filling my pants. My [thin] legs are now *big* legs. Don't know how my shoes got on such swollen feet, but there they are. One by one guys are falling asleep and drifting away from the raft never to be seen."

———

The chief yeoman who punched Luke Bobbitt in the face thirty minutes ago to revive him is now one of the dead. It's his place that Bobbitt takes on the raft. Soon after he's aboard the raft, he sees a young sailor swimming alongside. Years later Bobbitt will tell *Sea Classics* magazine, "He was out of his head. I grabbed him and he fought to get away. I couldn't hold him. One of his buddies was on the raft. I yelled, 'Grab him. He's getting away.' The fellow on the raft was paralyzed with fear. I belted him one. I said, 'You're his buddy. Get him.' He came out of it and went after him.

"He pulled him back but couldn't hold on. I grabbed the kid again. He was still fighting. He wanted to take off his life jacket. He kept screaming, 'Get your hands off me you bastards. I'm tired. Let me sleep.' I belted him in the face. I belted the living hell out of him. We pulled him onto the raft . . . I kept pounding the hell out of him. At least I thought I was . . . I didn't have much strength left."

Seaman 1/C Richard R. Novotny, from Riverside, Long Island, was the trunion operator of a 20mm gun on the *Leopold*'s starboard side almost directly above the spot where the 255's torpedo detonated. The explosion knocked him overboard, and he has been drifting in and out of consciousness ever since. But somehow he has latched onto a raft and is clinging to it with his right arm.

Like Nersasian and Bobbitt, Novotny's fortunate to be dressed in layers of clothing to insulate him against the cold. The lightly dressed cook hanging on the raft next to him is suffering badly. He keeps moaning that his legs hurt, his legs "are gone." Then like many of the dying men on the other rafts, the cook curls his hands into fists and starts swinging at Novotny. One punch nails him in the eye, another on the nose. Then, after the windmill of punches, the cook rolls onto his back and stares blankly at the moon and starts to drift away from the raft.

Novotny tries to grab him with his left hand, but he has no strength in his left arm. It's beginning to dawn on him that he really got hurt when the torpedo exploded. After he reaches a hospital in Northern Ireland he will be diagnosed with a shrapnel wound on the scalp, another on the left thigh, a severe compression fracture of the first and second lumbar spinal vertebrae, and a severe compression fracture of the second and third thoracic spinal vertebrae. Novotny is the most severely injured of all the Leo's twenty-eight survivors. He will spend almost six months in an Irish hospital, but he will live a long life.

Tonight he's not so sure. More and more men are drifting away from the rafts like the cook, dead. Yet from amid the floating corpses comes a voice of hope. The men on the rafts will never forget Lt. (jg) Robert J. Wescott bobbing by in the moonlight in his life vest shouting, "Hang in there, men. Don't give up."

CHAPTER TWENTY-NINE

Hard Decisions

March 9, 1944, 2120–2130 Hours

ERICH HARMS AND DIETER HENGEN SHUDDER. WHAT SEEMS LIKE A massive electric shock rockets through U-255, the backs of men's necks, their lungs, their hearts. Then they hear the thunder, the detonations. *Scheisse.* More depth charges? It seems that the enemy Feger that has been stopping and starting overhead for the better part of the last hour has found them at last.

Harms braces himself in the doorway to the hydrophone operator's booth, sees the Horch O rip off his headset in pain. He asks if the man is all right. Can he do his job or does he need a replacement? This is the classic script between skipper and Horch O after a depth charge explosion.

The Horch O's response is invariably the same. "*Jawohl, Herr Kaleun.*" All is well. Horch Os have been known to make such claims even when they are bleeding from an ear. Since these radiomen normally only have their headset over one ear at a time so that they can hear orders and questions in the boat, they usually just switch their earphone to their good ear after rupturing an eardrum. In the Ubootwaffe, even as late in the war as 1944, most men would rather die than shame themselves with a show of weakness. No one on this boat wants to be called a *Sitzpinkler*, a guy who sits to pee. U-boat culture is hyper-masculine.

Another explosion rocks the boat.

The Horch O says something's strange about what he's hearing from his hydrophones array, the GHG. It consisted of two sets of twelve hydrophones mounted on either side of the bow. The twenty-four hydrophones can hear single vessels up to twelve miles away and convoys up to sixty-five miles distant, depending on sea conditions. By measuring the time difference between each hydrophone's reception of the sound, the Horch O and his GHG can triangulate the location of the sound and get a fix on an enemy ship or convoy. Now he tells Harms that the explosions have detonated at a significant distance from one side of the boat, but the screw noises from the enemy Feger are much closer on the other side of the boat. And another thing. These explosions may not be from Wabos.

"*Was ist los?*" asks the skipper. What does this mean?

It means that the explosions could not have come from the Feger that they hear. And these explosions might be from something other than depth charges. Possibly there are two destroyers up there hunting them with more weapons than just depth charges, but the one that caused the explosions is stopped.

The U-boat Commanders Handbook can't help Harms in this situation. It says, *Accelerate your speed when the enemy accelerates his (or when depth charges are detonated); stop or crawl when the enemy stops.*

But now, with possibly two destroyers overhead, one steaming search patterns while another is stopped and launching explosives of some sort at God knows what, Harms is not sure whether he should take his cues to stop or start from the detonation of the depth charges or the stopping and starting of the Feger overhead. The ship overhead is his more immediate threat even though it has not attacked. The Americans' sonar has gotten very good at finding U-boats. It's not like the happy time off Norway when the English and the Americans seemed tone-deaf to the sounds of prowling sea wolves. It seems like the destroyers are playing a new game with Harms, and he knows that he better get creative with his defenses quickly or prepare to die.

And something else is causing a wrenching in his gut. The handbook says,

> On sighting convoys and other important objectives, in order that these may be attacked by other submarines as well, the submarine should report the sighting immediately, even before attacking itself,

and send further reports confirming the contact, in the intervals between its attacks on the enemy ships.

U-255 has sent out no radio transmission to BdU since this fiasco began. She has been too busy trying to hide, and Harms fears that sending even a brief "short signal" giving the convoy's position to U-boat Headquarters will allow the enemy's Huff-Duff to find him and kill him. The convoy is moving away at fifteen knots and may well have changed course since his fight with the first Feger. Unless he tells the Funker to send out the convoy's position soon, the other boats in wolfpack Preussen may never be in position to attack. The Allies' convoy of materiel will arrive safely in the British Isles, materiel to support an invasion of German-occupied Europe later in the spring. How will Admiral Dönitz feel about his delay in sending out a short signal? Is this delay a case of winning the battle but losing the war?

But none of this will matter if Harms lets his men die here and now. His best chance is to try to send the destroyer overhead chasing after a phantom, then try to run for it and hope he can get off a short signal to BdU soon.

"Prepare the BOLD," he tells his engineer.

BOLD is a metal canister about four inches in diameter launched through a special tube in 255. It holds calcium hydride, which gives off large quantities of gas when mixed with sea water. A valve in the canister allows the U-boat crew to determine the depth at which the BOLD deploys. To sonar, the gas bubble cloud resembles the sound signature of a submerged U-boat until the canister runs out of calcium hydride in about twenty minutes. However, since BOLD had come into widespread use in 1942, Allied sonar and sonar operators had gotten better at recognizing BOLD as a decoy. Still, the little canister is Harms's best hope for survival at the moment. That and a lot of luck.

"Release the BOLD," he orders.

He asks the Horch O for the course and speed of the Feger moving overhead, then he tells his helmsman to steer in the Feger's wake where it is hardest for the Allied sonar to detect him due to the water noise of the destroyer's wake. Motors ahead half.

CHAPTER THIRTY

Lord Have Mercy

March 9, 1944, 2120–2132 Hours

"WE'RE GETTING EXPLOSIONS, SIR." JOHN BENDER, THE ASW OFFICER, reports from the sound hut to Bob Wilcox on the bridge of the *Joyce*.

"From the sub?"

Bender says that he doesn't think so. The explosions sound like depth charges, but who knows for sure?

No one has to tell Wilcox what this means. The explosions must be coming from the *Leopold*. Quite possibly from her depth charges or maybe her torpedoes. These weapons may not have all been disarmed, and they are going off as she goes down. The fantail with its load of a hundred depth charges and three torpedoes is starting to sink, or already sinking. Maybe the sinking is causing explosions aboard. Maybe her magazines are erupting. Wilcox thinks about all those poor bastards from the *Leopold* who are in the water already. Goddamn. If he doesn't start rescuing them fast, there will be nothing but corpses in the water.

"Floater net off the port side. Men waving." The report comes from the lookouts' talker.

This is another one of those moments when Wilcox wishes he had a pipe of his Heines Blend and a moment to reflect, to imagine what his enemy down below is thinking and doing. He wonders if that U-boat commander knows that those exploding depth charges are just accidents ... or does he imagine that he's under attack? Does he think the *Joyce* has him in her sights? Or does he know that Wilcox has absolutely no god-

Capt. Robert Wilcox, commander
of the USS *Joyce* postwar.
COURTESY WILCOX FAMILY ARCHIVES.

damn idea where the U-boat is? Is he preparing to rise out of the gloom
and fire a retaliatory torpedo at the *Joyce* like the one that got the Leo?

At another moment Wilcox could get deeply into the psychology
of this game of cat and mouse. But the smoking light is out on the *Joyce*
and there's no time to reflect. He has to make a decision. Does he keep
searching for the U-boat or does he start saving the men that he can? His
mind tells him he would be a fool to slow the *Joyce* and make her a target.
Maybe his enemy is already setting up for a shot at him. The damn sonar
doesn't seem able to hear a thing except water noise and explosions. But
his heart tells him something else. There are men to save here. He can see
them now. His brother coasties are in the water and going through hell
in that cold, black sea.

"All stop," he says, then orders a course change to put the floater net
on his lee side to block the wind that could blow the net away. He tells
his crew to rig scramble nets to port and prepare to rescue survivors. Now
he can hear the men in the floater net shouting for help.

Wilcox holds his breath as the *Joyce* wallows in the swells. She's at a dead stop. The floater net is on the port side of the DE, rising and falling in six- to eight-foot seas.

I'm a goddamn sitting duck for that sub. That's the thought hammering at the back of the skipper's mind. "Get those men aboard," he shouts down to his executive officer who is overseeing the rescue.

On the deck of the *Joyce* men are heaving lines to the two guys in the floater net, but the castaways' hands are too frozen to hold on. So now the *Joyce* crew is heaving lines with nooses tied at the ends so the guys in the net can work the nooses around their bodies under their arms. Then the crew of the *Joyce* can haul them aboard like caught fish.

Fifty years later, shortly before his death in the mid-1990s, Bob Wilcox will give a video interview to filmmaker Rob Sibley and choke back tears as he tells the story.

"There were only two men in the floater net. We had them right alongside. There was a big fat guy. The floater net is mesh. And he had his leg trapped in the mesh and he couldn't get it out. We gave him twenty-one thread line. It's about as big as a finger. The other man in the net was the executive officer of the *Leopold*, named Mr. Cone. He tied the line around the other guy. Both of them had lines around them, both lines leading to our men on the deck. Our men were going over the side to help these guys, climbing down the cargo nets that we put over the side. At this time the lookout sang out, 'Torpedo.' This was on our port beam. 'Sounds,' sonar, picked it up in the sound gear. It sounds almost like a train in a tunnel. I ordered all ahead flank, full left rudder. And . . . a . . . it carried away the two men." Wilcox sobs. "Their lines broke."

In death Burtis P. Cone will receive the Navy and Marine Corps Medal in a ceremony in Richmond, Virginia. In a letter to his parents, Vice Adm. R. R. Waeshe, commandant of the US Coast Guard, wrote in recognition of the heroic courage of Lieutenant Cone: "His supreme courage reflected the true spirit of the Coast Guard and Naval Service."

Before this night is over Bob Wilcox will also earn a commendation, this one from the commander and chief, Atlantic Fleet. But Wilcox is not

Grave of Vice Adm. Russell R. Waesche, commandant of the US Coast Guard during World War II. COURTESY ROBERT NERSASIAN.

thinking about commendations or medals. He's thinking about the life and death of his ship and his men as the *Joyce* turns to face the torpedo. It is incoming from 320 degrees, which seems odd because this is more or less the same bearing as the wreck of the Leo's stern lying about fifteen hundred yards distant. When the first torpedo came at the *Joyce* from the port side an hour ago, the *Leopold's* stern was off to port then, too. Could the U-boat have surfaced or come up to periscope depth between the *Leopold's* stern and the *Joyce* twice and got off these shots? It would be a bold move indeed. The U-boat would be seriously risking exposing itself to the *Joyce's* lookouts as well as its surface-search radar, which is constantly watching the wreck of 317 and plotting its position. But neither the lookouts, nor the radar or sonar, have seen or heard anything until just now. As the *Joyce* turns, shouts rise from the men on the deck. They see the silvery wake of a torpedo—first, off to port, then crossing their stern.

Somewhere out there in the dark, things are going to hell on Sparky Nersasian and Luke Bobbitt's raft. The men in the raft have seen the *Joyce* stop as if intent on picking up men in the water, nets, and rafts. But then the *Joyce* raced away into the dark again.

"She's after the Jerrys," says someone. Who knows if she's ever coming back?

The men in the raft are up to their hips in water coming up through the grate in the bottom. They are feeling frozen from the waist down. Some urinate to try to keep warm. Others defecate. Every time a big wave washes over the raft, a few more guys slip overboard.

In Sparky Nersasian's words, "If you are five feet away from a man there is nothing you can do. You can't reach out and save him. He's gone. Three to four feet is the difference between living and dying. Two steps one way and you are saved. One step the other way and you are dead. He's looking at you and you think to yourself, 'He's dead.' There is nothing you can do. Can't even give him a hand. Sorry, you are dead. You have nothing left to give not even your hand." Like Wilcox, Nersasian will never be able to tell the story of this night without hitches in his speech, without stuttering, without snorting back the tears.

CHAPTER THIRTY-ONE

Night Songs

March 9, 1944, 2145 Hours

"DAMN IT."

The lights have just snapped off. To Jeremiah Bowen, Richard Forrester, and Gale Fuller, the fantail of the *Leopold* seems suddenly caught in a web of darkness. It's quiet except for the slap and rush of water. The auxiliary generator in the B4 engine room has finally flooded. Everyone who can picture the layout of 317 knows what's coming next. First sea water will start pouring into sick bay, then surge through the crew's berthing quarters, the petty officer's stateroom, the laundry. Then—with just the carpenter's shop and the steering gear room high and dry—the fantail will rise until the deck is nearly vertical. What's left of the Leo's stern will poise like a dart for a plunge more than a mile to the bottom of the ocean.

"Let me hear you sing, boys." Ensign Bill Tillman's shouting in the dark.

Almost instantly someone starts up with "Take Me Out to the Ballgame."

They follow this up with another upbeat favorite like the tune that Glenn Miller, the Andrews Sisters, and Cab Calloway have all recorded, "Chattanooga Choo Choo." It's a rousing song and Bowen, Forrester, and Fuller feel their blood begin to surge as they sing out into the dark with more than thirty of their shipmates.

Choruses of "Shortnin' Bread" and "Don't Sit Under the Apple Tree" make Forrester think about leaving his perch atop the stern light to get up and dance.

Bowen really belts it out when they sing songs like "The Daring Young Man on the Flying Trapeze" and "Don't Fence Me In."

For a while there's quiet on the fantail. The deck now has a 30-degree pitch forward. The K-gun launchers have slipped underwater.

These boys were the first generation to grow up with commercial AM radio and the record industry in America. Home radios have been ubiquitous virtually all of their lives and automotive radios have become standard in new cars. Radio is to Gale Fuller and his shipmates what the Internet will be to his great-grandchildren. Some stations like KDKA out of Pittsburgh, Pennsylvania, developed a national reach in the 1920s and soon syndicates like the National Broadcasting Company and the Mutual Broadcasting System were building networks of radio stations across the country and selling national advertising sponsoring shows like *The Lone Ranger, Superman,* and *Amos 'n' Andy.*

Walter Lee Ward, crewman of the USS *Leopold* who was lost at sea. COURTESY WARD FAMILY ARCHIVES.

While NBC is the broadcasting arm of radio manufacturer RCA, CBS has emerged as an outgrowth of record manufacturer Columbia Records, which started its network of stations with WROR in Newark, New Jersey, and a small Brooklyn station, WABC. Now, WABC has relocated to Midtown Manhattan, and CBS has built an empire that includes KCBS in San Francisco, KNX in Los Angeles, WBBM in Chicago, WCAU in Philadelphia, WJSV in Washington, DC, and well over fifty other affiliates. They all play music, a lot of music. Their own Columbia music. Columbia has signed recording stars like Al Jolson, Kate Smith, and Bing Crosby. And the *Leopold* has radio talent of its own. Sixty years later the family of Walter Ward will remember listening to him sing with a Coast Guard barbershop quartet on a radio station broadcasting from Radio City Music Hall in New York.

The boys on the *Leopold* and their cohorts who grew up with radio in the Depression love their music. They love the jazz of Duke Ellington, Louis Armstrong, and Jelly Roll Morton. The bebop of saxophonist Lester Young. The blues of Bessie Smith, Ma Rainey, and, especially, Billie Holiday, who records with Count Basie and Artie Shaw's orchestras. They listen to country and western music from the Grand Ole Opry via WSM in Nashville.

But what the guys like Sparky Nersasian and Luke Bobbitt on the *Leopold* really love is to swing-dance to the big-band music of bandleaders like Glenn Miller, Artie Shaw, Count Basie, Cab Calloway, Tommy Dorsey, Duke Ellington, and Benny Goodman. During the war years, young people by the millions are tuning in to coast-to-coast broadcasts of live swing music by Earl Hines and his Grand Terrace Cafe Orchestra. They feel their feet tap and their hips start to sway with the slurring hoots of saxophones and trombones in songs like "In the Mood," "Stompin' at the Savoy," "String of Pearls," and "Take the 'A' Train." The troops overseas get their swing from the Armed Forces Radio Service broadcasting from London and hosts like Tokyo Rose on Radio Japan.

The *Leopold*'s radio room, and U-255's Funkers, have a large selection of 10-inch and 12-inch, 78 rpm records to play over the vessels' PA systems to improve the crew's morale. Their daily fare of music is the swing songs and popular ballads by Frank Sinatra, Doris Day, and Ella Fitzgerald. Composers Frank Loesser, Cole Porter, Irving Berlin, Richard Rodgers, and Johnny Mercer are huge favorites.

So it is that tonight, under the stars on the sinking fantail of the Leo, the men grow somber as they harmonize about taking a sentimental journey. A hoarseness creeps into Gale Fuller's voice as he sings along to "I'll Be Seeing You." Both Billie Holiday and Bing Crosby have recorded the song this year. The voices must sound downright solemn as they sing songs like Jerome Kern's "Smoke Gets in Your Eyes." Imagine the wistfulness of these boys when they launch into Judy Garland's classic "Somewhere Over the Rainbow." Picture these sailors wishing with all their hearts that they could wake from this nightmare, fly far from this wrecked ship tonight to a land where troubles melt like lemon drops.

In the midst of the reverie the ship gives a terrible shudder, then pitches up almost on end. This is the last time Fuller, Forrester, and Bowen see their skipper Ken Phillips. He's too weak to hold onto the depth charge rack that he has been leaning against. He slips down the nearly vertical deck, free falls, hits the flak shield on the number three gun, and is gone.

So are more than a dozen other men. Vanished. When Tillman has the surviving men count off, there are only twenty-one of the original thirty-six left. Only forty feet of the fantail is still above the water and what remains has begun to look more like a steel pillar in the middle of the ocean than a ship.

There's a collection of large shoring planks at the very stern. Tillman says the men need to start building a raft. It's not over 'til it's over. From somewhere in the dark, a voice might well try to rally himself and his mates to action with the theme song from Kate Smith's popular radio show. The song is "God Bless America."

CHAPTER THIRTY-TWO

Settling Fast

March 9, 1944, 2218–2330 Hours

RICHARD FORRESTER'S CLINGING TO THE STERN LIGHT, THINKING, "I'M next." He has been watching wave after wave wash men off the fantail. But Ens. Bill Tillman's still aboard. He has a signal light, and he's sending a message blinking out in the direction where he last saw the *Joyce*. His Morse code spells out two words, "Settling Fast."

Only about fifteen feet of the ship remains above the water. The hull is almost vertical now, rudder in the air like a sail, and the wreck is rearing up and diving down with each wave. Wind and seas have been building since the Leo took the torpedo. The waves look like rolling hills with white, foaming crests. They cast harsh shadows in the intermittent moonlight. With his arms wrapped around the stern light, Forrester feels like he's riding a whale. When the stern plunges down into the North Atlantic, the waves break right over him. He has been counting. Seven waves have already rolled over him. Only he, Tillman, a bosun's mate, and a gunner's mate remain on the fantail. The wood for the raft that they hoped to build has been lost. The men pitched it over to guys who were swept into the water. The eighth wave rips him from the ship, tumbles him in the freezing sea. When he pops up, he heaves a deep breath and looks around. The stern is gone and so are Tillman and the others.

He's trying to float on his back as he was taught to do in the abandon-ship drills. His kapok life vest is doing a good job holding his head above the water. He can breathe pretty well if he keeps the breaking waves to his back. The water's cold, but he doesn't feel as wretched as he did clinging to the stern, alternately getting doused and then wind whipped. He's thinking that he just might make it if the 317 comes back to pick up survivors, when all of sudden something hits him like a massive electric shock. An explosion lifts him right out of the water about four feet. When he lands, his body is stinging all over. "Then there was a kind of gush," he will tell his interrogators at the naval board of inquiry. "It smoothed out all the water around there." Damn, he had been warned about just this kind of thing. Another one of the Leo's depth charges has detonated as the fantail sinks.

Gale Fuller and Jeremiah Bowen are blown into the air too. They were washed off the fantail just ahead of Forrester. Bowen will tell the board of inquiry that when the depth charge went off, "I was doubled up blowing up my life belt. My eardrums were perforated, and I was shaken up a little at the time. I was quite numb. I started swimming around, and about fifteen or eighteen of us found a plank and were holding on to it. They seemed to give up though and began to drop off. A fellow would take off his jacket and go down. Once I tried to help a fellow to the plank, but he was dead before I got there. The *Joyce* was still on the horizon, and we started to swim to it."

Fuller has found the plank too. As the other men drop off, Fuller and Bowen climb onto the plank. They start paddling and kicking toward the *Joyce* as if they are on a large surfboard. Now there are only three men left on the plank. Ensign Valaer of Washington, DC, is with Fuller and Bowen too. He's not paddling or kicking. He's just lying prone on the plank, hugging it, shivering all over. Fuller keeps telling the young officer that he needs to paddle and kick to keep up his circulation. But Valaer seems in a daze from the cold. Assigned on temporary duty to the *Leopold* only forty-eight hours before the ship sailed to fill in for a sick navigation and radio officer, Valaer was in the radio room when the torpedo struck and not dressed for the cold.

Crunched in the bottom of a slowly depopulating raft, and dozing in and out of consciousness from his injuries and the cold, Richard Novotny begins to hallucinate. Fifty years later, Novotny will tell an interviewer his story.

"I saw in life-size, and appearing to be alive, my loving wife of eight months, my wonderful mother and father, all standing in a row and looking down at me and smiling." The three figures stand in relief against a hazy background, which is in the shape of a perfect square framing his loved ones. The square, the hazy background, and the three people seem suspended about five feet above the crest of the waves. He feels no pain, feels at peace. There are times when he believes he crosses over to the other side—death—and then comes back.

Forrester's not sure, but he thinks at least one more depth charge goes off while he's in the water. It seems to detonate very deep and farther away. He pays little attention because he's totally focused on finding a raft or a plank to help keep him afloat. Neptune must be smiling on him because it's only a few minutes before he spots the silhouette of a raft pitching on the waves in the moonlight. With what's left of his strength, he swims toward it.

"What ship are you from?" shouts someone from the raft as he gets closer.

What the hell?

"Do you speak English?" Another question from the raft.

One of the guys in the raft raises a board over his head like a club.

Suddenly, Forrester gets the picture. The guys on the raft think he might be a German. They heard or felt the depth charges exploding, and they think that maybe the *Joyce* has nailed the sub that got the Leo. They sure as hell aren't going to share their raft with some damn kraut.

Forrester spits out his name, rank, serial number, and General Quarters assignment, K-gun number seven.

Bill Miller, Glyone Mahaffy, and Carl Graves help him aboard raft number four. It's not in good shape. The raft's floating upside down and packed with men up to their chests in water. Even as Forrester is being hauled aboard, the men on the raft are making room for him by easing the dead over the sides. Someone says he can see the 317. It looks like she's stopping to pick up survivors. Men start shouting, "Over here. Over here."

CHAPTER THIRTY-THREE

Angels

March 9, 1944, 2345 Hours–March 10, 0110 Hours

FOR THE LAST THREE HOURS THE MEN ON THE NUMBER FOUR RAFT have been trying to keep awake by singing. But now many of them are dead and the others are shivering so badly that the songs have stopped. After the *Joyce* left the area for the second time, a lot of guys seemed to give up hope. Some have taken off their life vests and slipped over the side. Forrester, Young, and Miller are among the few still alive. Barely. Someone told Warren Young that if he put his thumbs in the palms of his hands and holds them real hard, he won't feel cold. Now he's clasping his thumbs for all he's worth.

Bill Miller can't keep his focus on the raft and his shipmates any longer. He's started thinking about his baby brother Tommy who was born after he joined the Coast Guard and whom he has never seen. He had a chance to get home for a few hours before the Leo sailed on this trip, but he thought he would wait until he could get a little more time. He's imagining baby Tommy's pink little face now and saying over and over in his mind how sorry he is to Tommy. "I should have come home." You never know when you are going to run out of time.

It's while he's losing himself in regrets that someone—maybe Forrester, Mahaffy, or Graves—starts shouting in a hoarse voice. "Ship, ship."

Miller will tell the board of inquiry, "It came right up near us and went broadside. We were on the starboard bow, and they kept drifting over toward us. And it was rolling quite bad, and we got underneath the bow, almost straight down from her rail and forward deck. They threw the lines, two heaving lines. . . . They told us to tie it on the raft. They were going to haul us back aft to the side. Just about at that time the bow came up and it came down on the edge of the raft, twisted us all off. . . ."

One of the men who grabs the lines is Richard Forrester. As the raft capsizes he tries to hold onto the line, but it's slipping through his frozen hands. With a final burst of will he knots two half-hitches around one of his legs. The crew of the *Joyce* fish him aboard upside down.

Miller pulls himself back into the raft. There are only three other men aboard, including Warren Young, and the raft is drifting rapidly back along the port side of the *Joyce*. Miller can hear someone on the loudspeaker aboard the DE saying that the ship will be back. "Hold on."

"So we yelled a little, and they went away from us to their starboard . . . then they come around again, come around to starboard, swung right around. Their port was facing us broadside again, about, oh, I'd say one hundred yards away from us."

The rescue crew gathers on the port rail of the *Joyce* and shouts to the men in the raft to swim or paddle over to them, but the raft is upside down, and the men don't have a paddle, not even a board. So they scoop the water next to the sides of the raft with their hands until they are close enough that the men on the *Joyce* can throw them lines.

"I grabbed ahold of that, and I [tried to] tie it inside the raft there," says Miller. "I didn't make it. My hands were too cold to tie it. I remember Mahaffy was on the rope ladder there. We were rolling up and down quite a bit." Someone drops a loop over Miller's shoulder, a heavy line. He wiggles his arms above the loop of line so that it grabs him in his armpits. As the rescue crew hauls Miller up the side of the ship, he can't believe his luck, can't believe that he's still alive.

The rescue crew hauls aboard Warren Young too, upside down like Forrester. Sixty years later, he will remember, "They took me and another guy up to the officers' quarters and put us on the mess table. They stripped us down and put hot towels all over us. And they gave us whiskey. That helped. We were shivering so bad we were moving off the table." There is no doctor on the *Joyce*. The ship's pharmacist's mate Dan Kimball handles all the medical needs, and tonight he directs his assistants to position themselves around the wardroom table to make certain that guys like Young don't just shiver themselves off the table. Before the night is over, Kimball will perform miracles in reviving the rescued men, and his captain Bob Wilcox will recommend him for special commendation.

Sparky, brother Art, and author Robert, 1945. COURTESY ROBERT NERSASIAN.

Luke Bobbitt has never gone to church in his life, but now he's praying. Aloud. Encouraging others to join him. He and Sparky Nersasian's raft has found another raft. The two rafts are tied together. It's so cold that someone is dying every ten minutes when Bobbitt starts in on the Twenty-third Psalm. "The Lord is my shepherd. I shall not want. . . ." He's beginning to feel stronger, warmer, as the words flow from his mouth, as he hears his shipmates' voices saying that though they walk through the valley of the shadow of death, they will fear no evil "For thou art with me. . . ."

He's starting to picture God when he hears a low rumbling in the sky and the prayer fades from his lips.

"Do you hear that?" asks someone.

"It's a plane. Look."

A seaman points overhead. The aircraft is a four-engine Liberator bomber, an LRV. This one is Royal Air Force 157-L-4 from Iceland. It's circling the raft with an immense searchlight shining down at them. Now it's lighting up the sky with flares.

"They see us," says Bobbitt. "Keep praying, boys." He hugs the cross that he found in the water.

USS *Leopold*

Survivors of the sinking of the USS *Leopold*:

ANTONSANTI, Arturo; Sea2c

BOBBITT, Lucas Lee; Sea1c

BOWEN, Jeremiah James; EM3c

BOYCE, Henry Edward; Sea1c

BURGUN, Joseph Armand, SM3c

CHANDLER, Robert Elmer, Jr.; Sea1c

CHASTAIN, Norman Francis; F2c

DAUBE, Harry Milton; Sea1c

FOECKE, Roger M.; Sea2c

FORRESTER, Richard; TM3c

FREITAS, Antone, Jr., Sea2c

FULLER, Gale Lanteen; Sea2c

GOWENS, Troy Steve; Sea1c

GRAVES, Carl Mack; GM3c

HANYSZ, Joseph Max; MoMM2c

MAHAFFY, Glyone Robert; Sea1c

MILLER, William John; Sea1c

NERSASIAN, Nelson Jr.; Sea1c

NOVOTNY, Richard Robert, Jr.; Sea1c

O'BRIEN, William Gerard; Sea1c

PARKER, Cleveland Eugene; CCS

PIECHAL, Chester; Sea2c

REEVES, Clifford Charles; MoMM2c

SCHWARTZ, Herbert; RM3/c

SELAVONCHIK, Walter; Sea1c

SMITH, William Fredrick; SoM3c

SPINNING, Walter Lewis; Sea1c

YOUNG, Warren Blankenbiller; Sea2c

List of USS *Leopold* survivors. COURTESY USCG.

It takes a while but eventually the *Joyce* gets to the two rafts. Sparky Nersasian sees the cargo nets hanging over the side.

"I look up on the deck, and there's this big Italian with nothing but a skivvy shirt on and a rope around him. They are letting him down the side of the ship. He's grabbing guys one-handed. I got my life vest on, and the big guy asks me can I make it. I'm going to try. One by one, arm over arm, I just feel and get another wrung of the ladder. Finally two or three guys just grab me and throw me on deck like a caught fish.

"I'm lying on the deck freezing, and someone asks me what I would like. Who's got a shot?"

"Someone yells, 'Sparky, I got a shot for you.' I'm wondering who on the *Joyce* knows me. Here I am in the middle of the Atlantic, seven hundred miles from no place. It's my neighbor, Dr. Henry's son, Ensign Richard Henry. He went to MIT with my younger brother Arthur, and his father delivered my four siblings. Dr. Henry was the family doctor. What a coincidence. He hands me a half bottle of booze and says, 'Sparky, live it up.'"

Meanwhile, Luke Bobbitt has made it aboard, climbing the scramble net almost on his own. The adrenaline is pounding through his body as he reaches the deck. He looks up to the wing of the flying bridge, sees Bob Wilcox looking down with a serious face. Bobbitt thinks he'll say something to break everyone's tension, so he calls up to Wilcox, "How's the coffee on the *Joyce*?" Then he falls flat on his face.

When he comes to, he starts crawling around the deck on his hands and knees shouting for his friend. "Big John, Big John?"

"We got him," say the men on the *Joyce*. But they are just trying to keep Bobbitt calm as they cart him off to the wardroom for medical attention. Johnny Augsten has been lost like 170 of his shipmates.

CHAPTER THIRTY-FOUR

Escape

March 10, 1944, 0110–0230 Hours

OBERLEUTNANT ZUR SEE ERICH HARMS IS HAVING PROBLEMS. AND, AT the moment, he's too frustrated to be scared. At 2300 hours he heard the Feger that has been hunting him turn away on a northeast course. He waited another twenty minutes, then, when he was relatively sure that the destroyer was not coming back, he told his engineer to bring the U-boat to the surface. Hearing nothing on his hydrophones and seeing nothing on the moonlit seas, he finally tells his Funker that it's safe to send out a short signal to BdU. "Convoy [sector] AL17. U-255." But when twenty minutes on the surface pass without hearing any response from BdU, he orders the Funker to send the message again.

After yet another twenty minutes, he has still heard nothing. This is maddening. The convoy is getting away from U-255, and he has no evidence that BdU has received his reports or alerted the other boats in the wolfpack to converge on sector AL17. Feeling desperate to call in the wolves, Harms tells his Funker to send a standard radio message: "At 2200 [2000 hours on the *Leopold* and *Joyce*'s clocks, since the Germans and Americans set their ships' clocks to a different zero hour] convoy in naval grid square AK3862, course 070 degrees."

As Harms writes in his deck log that his third transmission has not been acknowledged either, he's feeling fatigued like everyone else in the crew from being on alert and hunted for more than four hours in the middle of the night. Perhaps he's just on the edge of feeling that he's alone out here and wishing that he were home in Bremerhaven with Marie and their four daughters when he hears Dieter Hengen, who has the watch on the tower, call down the voice pipe, "*Scheinwerfer* . . . searchlights, 180 degrees, distance five nautical miles." It's a plane.

Gott im Himmel. God in Heaven. Is this thing not over? Is the enemy still hunting him? With an aircraft now, one of their lethal "four-motors"? Harms can't hide the urgency in his voice as he orders the engineer to deploy a radar decoy called Aphrodite. But he doesn't dive the boat. He has a better chance of escape by running on the surface. His diesels can drive him at sixteen knots. Underwater his electric motors can only push him at about a third of that speed.

German romanticism and a poetical imagination seems to have been the impulse behind naming 255's radar decoy after the Greek goddess of love, pleasure, and beauty. The name Aphrodite means "foam arisen" or "foam born," and in the mythology surrounding her, she is always represented as having been born from sea foam as a young woman. Sandro Botticelli's Renaissance painting of her being carried ashore in a giant scallop shell has been plucking at the hearts of romantics for five hundred years, and it seems likely that some lovelorn staffer of the Kriegsmarine chose "Aphrodite" as the code name for a radar decoy because it rises from the sea to seduce Allied radar operators into thinking that they have spotted a U-boat.

First used by U-boats in the fall of 1943, Aphrodite is a hydrogen-filled balloon about three feet in diameter tethered to a raft launched from the deck of a surfaced U-boat like 255. The balloon floats a few feet above the waves. It is carried downwind of the raft on a tether of about 175 feet. Hanging from the tether are multiple strips of aluminum radar-reflecting tape. Aphrodite has a life span of three to six hours. After it is deployed, it gives off the appearance of a target quite like a surfaced U-boat on the radar screens of enemy hunter/killer aircraft like Royal Air Force 157-L-4 and ships like USS *Joyce*. As the Battle of the Atlantic rages on, seasoned Allied radar operators will learn to identify the Aphrodite decoy because it always points into the surface wind. But tonight the weapon is too new, and the radar operators on the *Joyce* and LRV are too inexperienced to quickly spot Aphrodite's ruse.

At 0135 hours, about twenty-five minutes after deploying Aphrodite, Hengen reports from the tower that the four-motor's searchlight is scouring the sea where Aphrodite is drifting. Harms notes this in his log. Part of him must sigh with relief that perhaps Aphrodite has done its job. She has bought him enough time to get about five miles away from the decoy. But part of him must feel worn down by this dance with the enemy. He has spent too many hours in the last three years aboard this old boat, trying to run and hide from the Allies. So now he probably steps out of the Zentrale and into the hazy darkness of the corridor outside the Funkers' cubicles so that none of his men will see him gritting his teeth and flexing the knobby horns of his jaw.

Once the crew of the LRV sees Aphrodite with their searchlight and realizes they have been fooled, the four-motor will likely widen its search pattern . . . unless it is helping a Feger to search for the crew of the ship 255 torpedoed. Maybe for just a second Harms's mind begins to picture a lot of men freezing in the icy waters, begging their god for salvation. But this is not the time for dark thoughts or sympathy. That will come later, he knows, if and when he ever can find the time to return to his berth and close these eyes that are burning from fatigue, the fumes of diesel exhaust, and fear. Now he must do everything he can to protect his men and give the Fatherland more victories to ward off a national sense of impending doom.

Even though the Nazi government tries to hide the details of the devastating bombing that Germans are suffering, Harms has heard about it from Marie in her letters. Back in November waves of Allied bombers hit Bremen and Bremerhaven with massive raids. The worst was on November 26 when over five hundred B-17s and B-24s pounded the port and the city to pieces. Before the war ends over six hundred thousand German civilians will die in the raids, including seventy-five thousand children. On one night in July of 1943, Allied bombs and the resulting firestorm kill forty-five thousand people in Hamburg. Harms fears for Marie and his daughters every day. Convoys of tankers, like the one that he's chasing, are bringing aviation gas to Allied bombers in England. The convoys are making such mass killing possible. He must do what he can to stop it no matter the cost to his boat and men, no matter how exhausted the machine, the crew, and he are at the moment.

He has already told his engineer to have 255's diesels thumping away at maximum revolutions. The engines have been far from flawless during the trip from Norway. Everyone on the boat can smell the tart scent of overheating lubricants wafting through their iron cocoon. Harms prays that now is not the time that his engines choose to develop serious compression problems, snap a rod, or burn a bearing. There is still the convoy to try to locate and shadow, still the wolfpack to call in for the hunt if he can. This is his duty.

As it says in the U-boat captain's handbook:

The success, or otherwise, of the attacks of all the other submarines operating against the convoy depends on the skill of the first submarine, whose duty it is to keep the contact with the convoy.

Elsewhere in the handbook it reads:

Failing orders to the contrary, the most important thing always is to attack. Each submarine should be concerned primarily with carrying out its own attack. Exceptions, for example, for boats whose task it is to maintain the contact with the convoy, must be in accordance with orders from Headquarters.

Where are those orders from headquarters? Why in God's heaven has BdU still not acknowledged his radio transmission? Does it not want him to shadow this convoy? Does it simply want him to catch up with it and attack again? Is sinking a destroyer not enough for Admiral Dönitz? Must U-255 hunt down every fat tanker that Harms can find and blow it to pieces? Or is he getting no answer from BdU because something has gone afoul with his transmitter, receiver, or antenna?

Verdamit. He has already asked the Funkers to check their sets and the deck crew to inspect the boat's antennas, but now he wants them to do it again. *Mach schnell.* On the double. Then he's going to submerge to hide from that four-motor bee, to wait for a message from BdU and listen for the convoy. It's his supreme hope that this battle with the two Fegers has run its course, his supreme hope that he can bring this old boat home safely. If and when that happens, if and when this war ends, he knows that he will have to reckon with the souls of the men he sent to heaven tonight. This is the knowledge that comes between him and eating, the knowledge that has turned him skeletal thin. As 255 dives below the surface, the dead seem to be gathering all around this U-boat.

CHAPTER THIRTY-FIVE

Last Men

March 10, 1944, 0230–0248 Hours

"TRIAL BY FIRE." THIS IS HOW LT. (JG) HARRY H. HAM JR. OF AUBURN-dale, Massachusetts, might well describe his night leading rescue operations aboard his ship. Ham is the first lieutenant on USS *Joyce*, and he has been in charge of rescue operations since the moment that Bob Wilcox saw the Leo folding up on itself shortly after taking the torpedo.

Trying to rescue her crew has been anything but a by-the-book operation. Early in the rescue Ham, executive officer Lt. Kingdrel Ayres, and Bob Wilcox decided that with the *Joyce* rolling 15 degrees port and starboard in these building seas, it would be too dangerous to launch the motor whaleboat and that it was not equipped to help with the rescue anyway. All the rescue operations had to originate from the main deck of the *Joyce*.

During the initial rescue attempts, Ham has seen a lot of shouting, individual sailors from the *Leopold* bobbing in the water, so many that his ship has had a difficult time maneuvering among them . . . let alone picking them up. By all accounts the *Joyce*'s exec Kingdrel Ayres is a very capable ship-handler, and he has been conning the *Joyce* most of the time since the *Joyce* began trying to pick up survivors. But it has been far from easy. As if darkness, building seas, and increasing wind are not enough to challenge the captain, every time he brings his ship to a full stop, she starts drifting at about two knots, pushed by the wind. This drifting is making it extremely difficult to get a 306-foot, fifteen-hundred-ton ship alongside floating individuals in the water, especially when trying not to run over other men. Furthermore, it's clear that with the ship drifting as she does, men can only be picked up on the lee side of the vessel where the ship acts as a wind break to keep the men in the water from being blown away.

As if nature's challenges are not enough, the two torpedo attacks on the *Joyce* have put everyone on edge and disrupted any sustained effort at rescue for hours. Losing Pete Cone and the cook during the first attempt to pick up survivors has been heartbreaking for Ham. He knows that for the rest of his life, in his dreams, he will see that look of blighted hope in Cone's eyes when the *Joyce* went to flank speed, pulling him like a caught fish until the twenty-one-strand line snapped and left the Leo's exec to drown.

But Ham and John Bender, who has left the sound hut to join Ham and four boatswain mates, have rallied and improvised. They have strategically placed groups of rescuers on both sides of the ship's waist and another group in the bow, all manned by repair parties, gunners, and ammo handlers. Since the accident with Pete Cone, they have learned that most of the *Leopold*'s survivors do not have the strength to climb the scramble nets hanging over the side. The rescue parties have also learned that the twenty-one-strand line is insufficient for lifting a man out of the water. Ham has had his men replace the twenty-one-strand throw lines with two-inch rope, each with a three-foot noose tied at the end. In the last two hours Ham and his crew have rescued more than twenty men with these nooses.

He's in a battle against time and nature. Time is running short for the men in the water. It's amazing that any of them are still alive in the frigid sea and the cold air. By most scientific reckoning all of these men should have perished hours ago. Still, the *Joyce* and the LRV keep finding small pockets of survivors among the ghastly congregations of floating corpses. The worst seem to be tangled in the floater nets that were supposed to save their lives. The living men in the water are so frozen that they can't even pull the nooses over their shoulders. Just adding the heavier line and the nooses has not been enough to make for quick and effective survivor recoveries, and every second counts.

In the recovery of survivors like Sparky Nersasian, the rescuers have realized that they must put men from the *Joyce* in the water. And so they are. With every rescue attempt now, Ham is sending volunteers tied in ropes—like Barney Olsen from Staten Island, New York—down to help the men in the water. Seventy years later, Olsen will say, "When I went down into the water, I wondered if I would come back. When I did, it was with a dead guy. Some of this stuff I haven't talked about. But I dreamt about it for a long time."

For their efforts in the rescue, for risking their lives by going overboard to recover the survivors of the *Leopold*, Barney Olsen and ten other men from the *Joyce* will receive the Navy and Marine Corps Medal.

Waldron Chastain

Charles Friend

Eugene Groene

Elmer Harris

Patrick Irwin

Roy Nelson

Wilbur Smith

William Smith

George Vann

J. E. Young

Their award is the highest noncombat decoration given for heroism by the US Navy to the members of the Navy and United States Marine Corps.

On the deck of the *Joyce* tonight, none of these heroes gives this improvised practice a second thought. But when the story of the recovery airs before a board of inquiry a month later, Navy and Coast Guard officials will take note of Ham's improvised solutions that saved lives. His choice to put rescuers in the water is the forerunner of the twenty-first-century

Coast Guard's standard practice of deploying a rescue swimmer to help in recovering shipwrecked mariners.

———

The last two men alive of the eighteen men who grabbed onto the shoring plank when the fantail sunk, Gale Fuller and Jeremiah Bowen, are so cold and so soaked with saltwater and oil from the *Leopold* that they can barely see. They are so tired that they don't even share their names with each other. But they keep spitting out the sharp-tasting fuel oil and paddling their plank toward the silhouette of the *Joyce* until the dark, steel side of the ship appears like a wall in front of them and someone shouts, "Hang in there, buddies, I'm coming for you."

A life ring on a rope lands next to the plank. Then a rescuer with a line tied around him drops into the water and wraps nooses around each of the men.

Bowen gets hauled aboard first, then Fuller. They are both laid on stretchers, covered with blankets, and whisked off to pharmacist's mate Dan Kimball.

Bowen will tell the board of inquiry, "I came to in the wardroom. They were trying to revive me. I went out again and came to in the first lieutenant's bed."

Fuller is out of it too; all he remembers of his rescue is waking up on the wardroom table and hearing someone say, "Set the war cruising watch."

Both men are only vaguely aware that Dan Kimball has brought them back to life with shots of stimulants, mouth-to-mouth resuscitation, heated towels, and body massages with warm oil.

———

For hours Richard Novotny has continued to drift in and out of consciousness, but he wakes to the sounds of his two raft mates shouting. Their raft is just about to smack up against the port side of the *Joyce*, when the ship takes a roll so hard to starboard that he sees the keel, part of the port propeller, and rudder.

"This is it," he thinks. The ship is going to roll back on top of him.

But it doesn't. He looks up and sees sailors in heavy weather gear gathered all along the ship's rail. Men tied in ropes are already climbing down the scramble nets to rescue his mates and him. He watches in a daze as the rescuers from the *Joyce* sling two of his mates into nooses and haul them up the side of the ship to the main deck. Now it's his turn. He's on the far side of the raft from the ship, so he tries to move across the raft toward the *Joyce* and the men coming down the scramble net. This is when he discovers that he cannot move. He has absolutely no control of his body from the hips down. His back has been so wracked from the initial torpedo explosion that threw him overboard that he can barely keep his head and chest above water.

The raft has begun to drift away from the ship, just a foot or two, but this could be the difference between life and death. Then just at this moment, here comes a man from the *Joyce* who seems to be flying down the scramble net with a two-inch line over his shoulder. Almost instantly the rescuer is in the water with him. He feels the noose wrap under his arms. Then both he and his rescuer are in the air, dangling against the side of the ship as men on deck pull them up to the deck, grunting the chant "Heave, heave, heave." Guys get him over the lifeline, stand him up, and remove the noose. They figure he's okay to try to stand on his feet.

"I crumple to the deck like a sack of potatoes," he will tell his interviewer Lewis Andrews Jr. in 1991. "I do not know how to explain adequately my feeling about Chuck Friend who was the *Joyce* crewman who put the line under my arms at the risk of his own life. I will never stop appreciating the heroism and the great all-out effort that Captain Robert Wilcox, his officers and men . . . put forth."

Sailors put him on a stretcher and take him to the crew's berthing area near sick bay. The next thing he knows he's on the bottom berth of a three-tier stack of bunks. His clothes have been stripped off. At first, he feels that welcome warmth of hot blankets being placed all over his body. Then comes the horrendous pain of his spinal injury. Pharmacist's Mate Kimball is at his side as the pain starts to blind him. Almost instantly, Kimball hits him with a big shot of morphine and its "Sleep tight, Richard." When he's lost in the lavender haze of the opiate, Kimball cleans and stitches up shrapnel wounds on Novotny's forehead and left thigh before moving on to the next man who needs him.

It's almost 0245 hours when the *Joyce* with the help of the LRV's search-light accounts for all of the *Leopold*'s floater nets, each snarled with the dead, and locates the last of the Leo's four rafts. Three of the men brought aboard—Bennie Porter, Edridge Cooper, and Ernie Larson—can't be revived. They are doubled over and frozen like grotesque statues. But one, Joseph Armand Burgun, who has been cradling the frozen Larson for hours, is still alive, still singing songs to the dead. A signalman, a man Burgun knew from the *Joyce*, jumps in the water and pulls the raft to the cargo net of the *Joyce*. When Burgun is hauled on deck at 0248, he becomes the last of the *Leopold*'s crew to be rescued. He has been in the water since 2130 hours. He has survived more than five hours in the 47-degree water. He will spend six weeks in an Irish military hospital recovering from the damage caused by hypothermia, a broken leg, and a belly full of shrapnel. Experts in the field of cold-water immersion will call his survival unprecedented, miraculous, inexplicable. The capacity of the human spirit, they will say, is beyond measure.

CHAPTER THIRTY-SIX

Nightmares

March 10, 1944, 0750–0850 Hours

LT. (JG) HARRY HAM FEELS LIKE HELL. HE'S THE OFFICER ON DECK ON the forenoon watch aboard the *Joyce*. After less than three hours of sleep, he's not sure if he's coming or going. Before he relieves John Bender on the flying bridge, he stands at the small drop-leaf chart table on the steering bridge of the O2 deck and reads Bender's summary of the morning watch, which is ending, in the log.

At 0446 hours the crew of the ship finally secured their vessel from General Quarters and the men not on watch then, like Ham, could finally get some rest. Bender's summary goes on to list the twenty-eight survivors. In a separate paragraph Ham reads, "The dead were as follows. . . . Death was certified by Commanding Officer. Cause of death: exposure."

The names of the dead—Bennie Porter, Edridge Cooper, and Ernie Larson—swim before his eyes in the red, night-vision light that is on over the chart table. Suddenly, he's reliving the horror of last night all over again. He's down on the main deck in the dark with a gang of men pulling Sparky Nersasian over the rail by his legs with his teeth chattering. He's wrapping blankets around Luke Bobbitt, who is shivering so badly that he's flopping off a stretcher. He's seeing the broken body of Richard Novotny do a face plant against hard steel. The frozen corpses of Bennie Porter and Edridge Cooper appear out of thin air doubled over and frozen like statues of trolls, not men.

Then he's looking into a swamped raft where Armand Burgun is cradling Ernie Larson in his arms. Larson is obviously dead. There is a coating of frost on his cheeks, but Burgun is still singing to him. Ham can hear the lyric twisting through his brain, over and over again like torture. Seventy years later he will say that it sounded like "Don't sit under the apple tree with anyone else but me. . . ."

"Message from Virgil coming in, sir." The voice of the bridge talker draws Ham back to the world of the living.

Now what?

Commander Task Group 21.5, Captain Kenner on the *Poole*, has ordered USS *Joyce* to sink the partially submerged bow of the *Leopold* in order to eliminate this navigational hazard for future convoys.

Without remembering climbing the ladder to the O3 deck, Ham finds himself on the flying bridge looking for what is left of the *Leopold*. He's cradling a bone-colored mug of strong black coffee between his mittens, gulping what the crew calls "rocket fuel" to bring himself out of the shadows. As he squints toward the west in search of the wreck, he surveys the weather conditions and sea state to write in the deck log. This is not an intentional act. Ham's running mostly on automatic responses. His mind may well still be partially trapped under the apple tree with Armand Burgun and poor, dead Ernie Larson. The temperature is 42 degrees, winds eleven to fifteen knots out of the southwest, seas moderate, the sky gray with scudding clouds, visibility eight miles.

"Bow of the *Leopold* . . ." says the lookouts' talker. Ham doesn't catch the bearing. Doesn't see the wreck yet. But good God Almighty, he must call the men to General Quarters yet again . . . this time to sink what's left of a sister ship. This time he's staying up here on the flying bridge where things feel safe. It's 0810 hours.

—◆—

"I'm not sure you want to see this, skipper," says Ham, but Bob Wilcox is already pulling his trusty Mark 28 Bausch & Lombs to his eyes and following the gaze of the other men on the bridge who have their binoculars trained on the floating bow section of the *Leopold*.

Robert Wilcox with pipe.
COURTESY WILCOX FAMILY ARCHIVES.

Unlike Ham, Wilcox feels exceedingly wide-awake. Since the *Joyce* hauled the last of the survivors aboard a few hours ago, he has been resting in his winter deck gear on the day bed at the after end of the steering bridge. Maybe he slept, but probably not. He's still juiced on adrenaline. His mind is ticking through all the things he has to do to keep his men safe today, including trying to resolve the problems with the radar and sonar. Then he must prepare to bury three men of the *Leopold* at sea. What passage should he read from the Bible?

Alert as Wilcox feels, Ham is right, the skipper sure as hell doesn't like what he's seeing as he focuses his binoculars on the bow of the *Leopold* bobbing three hundred yards to starboard. Later at the board of inquiry in New York, Wilcox will simply say there was a man dangling from the port anchor. He will not say he remembers every detail. He will not say that from a distance the bow section of the *Leopold* pointed to the sky like a mirage of an Egyptian pyramid rising out of the sea. He will not say that the wreck was floating bow high and listing over to starboard. Nor will he say that he saw chief quartermaster Richard Leo Graham hanging upside down, with his right leg caught below the knee between the shank of the big gray anchor and one of the flukes. He will not say that Graham was wearing his boots, jungle pants, a dark blue denim winter deck jacket but no woolen watch cap. No mittens.

But these are the details that will sear the memories of Wilcox, the lookouts, and the other men on the flying bridge of the *Joyce*. They see Graham's dark hair frozen over his forehead. The eyes are bulging wide open as if to say, "Holy shit," as if he has discovered that war and life itself are cosmic jokes. What the hell, you might as well find some nifty way to die.

"Goddamn it." Wilcox is muttering his favorite curse under his breath. "Just goddamn it all to hell."

What he wouldn't give right goddamn now for a pipe of Heines Blend with a little Amphora. Or better yet a stiff gin and tonic. He pulls the binoculars away from his face and looks down from the flying bridge. Dozens of men are scrambling to their battle stations. They don't seem real. He feels like he is watching a movie. Each man is wearing boots, jungle pants, dark deck jackets. Each is looking way too much like that dead fellow hanging from the Leo's anchor.

Oh brother, for a pipe! He really learned to love it when he was in the *Modoc* following the night she got fired on by the *Bismarck*. That was the night the *Bismarck* sunk the *Hood* in the Denmark Straits and she went down in three minutes, losing 1,418 of 1,421 men. It was after that cruise when he really started to enjoy gin. For the rest of his life he will love his pipe. Everyone who knew Bob Wilcox will remember how much he loved the ritual of his daily "cocktail hour" and his gin. But now, just like last night when he craved his pipe, the smoking light is out. And, of course, there's no drinking alcohol for recreation on an American warship. Heads up, skipper. Your ship and her crew are at General Quarters. These are combat conditions. Again. Still.

Wilcox eyes the dead man on the *Leopold*. He paces back and forth from one side of the flying bridge to the other, trying to keep his fearless leader face on, trying to think what David Farragut would do here. No human being should see this. How can he shoot at the wreck with that man hanging there? After all, that man was a brother. The skipper of the *Joyce* does not know yet that the chief was a hero. It will be decades before anyone realizes that Graham was the chief who counseled men on the bow like Sparky Nersasian and Luke Bobbitt on how to get over the side safely, the one who stayed behind until the last man was down the rope.

Abruptly, Wilcox sees what he must do and gives the order to circle the wreck. He will not fire on Chief Graham. At 0819 hours after the dead man is out of sight, Wilcox tells his 20mm gunners on the starboard side to open fire at the waterline on the wreck to sink it. He tells the crew on the three big 3"/50 deck guns to commence firing too. But after ten minutes being pounded by artillery, the bow of the *Leopold* shows no signs of sinking. The *Joyce*'s starboard 20mms are sizzling, so he turns his ship around and opens fire with the port guns, including the 40mms now. Still, the *Leopold* refuses to sink.

"Prepare to launch depth charges," says Wilcox. No doubt he's thinking something like "Damn the torpedoes. Full speed ahead."

***

Sparky Nersasian shudders in his berth. He can hear the sound of heavy gunfire, the 3"/50s booming, the 20mms and 40mms pounding away. Maybe this is a dream, more like a nightmare, he thinks, because it is all happening again.

He hears his gun captain Fran Bradley barking at Luke Bobbitt to load another shell on the double. He is trying to adjust the elevation on his gun when he feels a shock wave, like an electrical jolt, rock him. Then he notices that the poc-poc-poc of the 20mms has stopped. His ears ache, and his headset has gone dead.

"Oh, Christ, Jerry," says someone.

Jerry Claus sits hunched over in his seat, still strapped to the 3"/50. He can't talk, is barely moving. The left side of his face is slick with blood. In fact, his left eye is closed and his left cheek and the left side of his jaw are missing. His remaining teeth are brilliant white and streaked with blood. Undistinguishable words are gurgling from his throat.

Sparky Nersasian's still trying to shake the nightmare image of Claus's face, when he hears Luke Bobbitt tell him to wake up and put on a life vest. The shit has hit the fan again. Jesus Christ, it must be another U-boat circling for the kill. Instinctively, his right hand goes to the breast pocket of his shirt and feels for his pack of Chesterfields, but then he realizes that he is wearing borrowed clothes. Who the hell knows where he can find a butt?

He's still freezing. As he opens his eyes, he sees that his hands are shaking as they fumble to pull the wool blankets up around his shoulders. Jesus, what's wrong with him? He's wondering if this flashback and the shivering is the aftermath of severe hypothermia or is it what the military called at the time "shell shock" or "combat fatigue." To hell with it. He's not going anywhere. He thinks about music for relief, Puccini's aria "Nessun Dorma" once more.

Vanish, o night!
Fade, you stars!
At dawn, I will win!
I will win! I will win!

Although he's buried too deep in his blankets to notice, at 0854 hours, after taking two depth charges from the *Joyce*, his once-gallant ship and his number two gun finally sink.

— ⚓ —

According to the Anxiety and Depression Association of America (ADAA), what the US military began calling "shell shock" during World War I is today known as post-traumatic stress disorder (PTSD). It "is a serious potentially debilitating condition that can occur in people who have experienced or witnessed a natural disaster, serious accident, terrorist incident, sudden death of a loved one, war, violent personal assault such as rape, or other life-threatening events."

Three main types of symptoms characterize PTSD. One common symptom is like Nersasian's re-experiencing his trauma through distressing flashbacks and nightmares. A second symptom is Ham's feeling of being in a daze. He feels emotionally numb, and he wants to stay up on the flying bridge where he feels safe. He feels a need to avoid a place like the main deck that reminds him of the faces of the dead men whom he could not save. A third symptom is a sense of increased arousal. In such a situation a person has difficulty sleeping and concentrating and is hyper-vigilant like Bob Wilcox when he comes on deck. He feels jumpy and easily irritated, angry.

One solution to relieving the symptoms of PTSD is to escape the stressful situation. But on a ship in combat conditions in the middle of the North Atlantic, there is no physical way to escape. In such situations many people, when possible, turn to chemical escapes like drugs and alcohol. Like Sparky craving his cigarettes this morning on the *Joyce*—like Bob Wilcox dreaming of his pipe and a gin. Both Wilcox and Ham feel detached as if the other people around them are actors in a film. They no longer feel, no long hear the pleading of the wounded, smell the scent of dead men soaked in fuel oil.

But this morning on the *Joyce* Nersasian and Ham are not suffering from PTSD. According to the ADAA, to have PTSD a person must experience symptoms for at least one month following a traumatic event. At the moment Nersasian and Ham are experiencing a condition that may be a precursor to PTSD known as acute stress disorder. ASD roots in the same traumatic experiences that cause PTSD, but the symptoms may subside quickly. Only time will tell.

"It's not unusual for people who have experienced traumatic events to have flashbacks, nightmares, or intrusive memories when something terrible happens—like the 9/11 terrorist attacks and those in cities around the world (Orlando and Paris, for example) or the bombings at the 2013 Boston Marathon, or active combat," says the ADAA. "Most people who experience such events recover from them, but people with PTSD continue to be severely depressed and anxious for months or even years following the event." Sufferers may develop obsessive relationships with their de-stressor of choice for the rest of their lives. In this regard, Sparky Nersasian will become a chain smoker. Eventually, he will die of lung cancer. Except for his narrative on his niece Tory's tape, he will almost never talk about March 9, 1944. For many years after the loss of the *Leopold*, he will refuse to swim in the ocean or even a pool.

Sparky Nersasian was far from alone among his cohort of vets suffering from PTSD. According to research for the PBS show *Perilous Fight*, "One in four World War II casualties was caused by 'combat fatigue.' For those in lengthy, intense fighting, the ratio was one in two. In the Pacific, where combat fatigue was most prevalent, 40 percent of 1943 evacuations were 'mental.' Twenty-six thousand psychiatric cases were reported just from Okinawa. To keep sailors from going mad anticipating kamikaze attacks, they weren't alerted to approaching planes until they absolutely had to be."

———

At about 0840 U-255 is running on the surface in grid AL 1858 when the Horch O tells Erich Harms he hears sounds—possibly a depth charge, possibly the sounds of a Feger's propellers too.

"Alaaaarm," calls the skipper down the voice pipe from the bridge, "Crash dive." He drops below and closes the tower hatch after him.

The jangling bell calling the crew to battle stations is still ringing as he drops down the ladder to the control room. Men are still bolting forward through the Zentrale to move the crew weight forward and accelerate the dive, as Harms swipes dripping sea water off his brows and cheeks.

With the boat now shifted to quiet electric motor power and running below the surface, the Horch O has a better chance of assessing the sounds that he hears in his headphone.

"They are far off," he says, "bearing about 070 degrees." Perhaps he has just heard another explosion like a depth charge.

Harms must be wondering who the Americans are trying to kill now? Who is dying? Are they still looking for him? Are the Yanks ever going to let him out of their grip? This is one of those moments when he pictures being stuck on the bottom in a wounded boat. He can imagine being trapped in this fetid, damp pipe . . . with the air reeks of oil, sausage grease, unwashed armpits, *Scheisse*—human waste. He can smell the acrid scent of men's fear. Water is rushing into to the boat through vulnerable spots like the air induction vents for the diesels and the seals for the prop shafts. Lights snap out.

He can hear the incessant sound of running water, so much water that the U-boat is becoming too heavy to lift off the seabed. Ever. And the Wabos keep on coming. This is when he remembers other times when he has nearly been blown to pieces or suffocated out of existence. This is the moment he thinks he can hear his shipmates coughing, wheezing, and gagging. He can smell them retching from a lack of oxygen as they suffocate or drown. This is the old U-boatman's nightmare of Blechkoller, a fear of depth charges and a form of PTSD specific to U-boat crews.

Despite BdU's counsel about running on the surface in broad daylight, *Tageslicht*, he tells his engineer, "Take her up again." He will not drown down here like a rat. And when he surfaces he will be prepared for anything. "Arm all remaining eels, gun crews at the ready."

Harms is not a man like Harry Ham or Sparky Nersasian suffering a first encounter with the precursors of PTSD, not even a man like the captain of USS *Joyce* who masks his PTSD beneath a mask of gallantry. This is a man who can only repress his full-blown PTSD by sheer will, hyper-vigilance, and the urge to forever run away.

CHAPTER THIRTY-SEVEN

Moving Forward

1944–2010

IN A HOST OF WAYS, THE SINKING OF USS *LEOPOLD* WILL HAUNT THE lives of all the men who survived the nightmare of March 9–10. In the days following its escape from the *Joyce* and the LRV, U-255 will run afoul of another LRV. On the night of March 11, while still searching for convoys to attack, Erich Harms's U-boat will be caught on the surface. The LRV will make three low-level bombing and strafing attacks on 255. Two men from the submarine will be injured by enemy gunfire, one severely. BdU will order Harms to rendezvous with U-608, which has a doctor. But the weather will be too rough and the meeting with the doctor will never take place.

Superstitious and religious men on 255 will wonder if the air attack and the failure to meet 608 for medical aid are signs of divine retribution for the men who have surely died aboard the yet-unknown destroyer they torpedoed on March 9. Eventually, 255 will head to her new base in France, barely escaping devastation by another air attack from British Mosquito bombers as it tries to enter the U-boat base at St. Nazaire, France.

After the safe return Admiral Dönitz will congratulate Erich Harms in person for a successful cruise and BdU will write for the record:

The boat assigned up to now in the [European] North Sea has proven itself well on its first Atlantic enterprise. The convoy was energetically and purposefully attacked, the destroyer paid for forcing the boat away

with its sinking. The aircraft attacks were repelled successfully. The crew adapted to the new combat conditions and proved itself.
Accredited success: 1 destroyer sunk.

By the standards of U-boat victories set near the beginning of the war when U-boat aces like Harms's mentor Reinhart Reche could claim five or more Allied ships sunk per patrol, 255's eighth patrol is a modest accomplishment. But by the measure of U-boat patrols in 1944, when only one in five boats makes it back to its base, Harms's crew has good reason to celebrate. To remember the success, Dieter Hengen will take pictures of the celebration on the dock when the beer, the wine, and the whiskey are flowing. And he will take a picture of Erich Harms receiving congratulations from Karl Dönitz. By contrast, 255's sister ship, U-986, the boat nearest to Harms when he battled the *Leopold*, will be lost with all hands just two days away from her base, probably after an air attack like the ones 255 dodged.

During the next thirteen months, 255 will leave on five more patrols but will always return to base within days of leaving with mechanical problems or under cryptic orders from BdU. She will never see battle again, but she will be one of the few U-boats to survive the entire war. Following the German surrender in early May 1945, her captain will give her up to the British navy in Scotland. Under Operation Deadlight to eliminate Germany's latent military capacity following the German surrender, she will be towed into the ocean southwest of Ireland. On December 13, twin-engine Beaufighters of Royal Air Force Squadron 54 will use her for target practice, sinking the tired old hulk with RP-3 rockets.

Shortly after retuning to St. Nazaire, Dieter Hengen, the 1WO aboard 255, will leave 255 to become the skipper of a new type XXI boat, one of the Third Reich's super weapons. These boats are the first submarines designed to spend most of their cruising life underwater. They can travel submerged for three days and outrun many surface ships. They can load and fire eighteen torpedoes in twenty minutes. After the war they will become the prototype for the modern submarines of the US, Soviet, and British navies.

The crew of U-255 partying in port. COURTESY OF DEUTSCHES U-BOOT MUSEUM CUXHAVEN.

Hengen will not see combat again, but he will never forget the sinking of the *Leopold* nor Erich Harms. Over the decades following the war, he will submit a lot of memorabilia, including his pictures of U-255's homecoming and Harms with Dönitz to the Deutsches U-boot Museum in Cuxhaven.

Erich Harms will not remain much longer aboard 255 either after sinking the *Leopold*. He will return to Germany for retraining as a skipper of a type XXI U-boat. Following spending some time with his wife and four girls, as well as training, Harms will take command of U-3023 in January 1945. Neither he nor his new U-boat will see battle, but they will have a heroic moment. As eastern Germany falls to the Red Army during the early spring of 1945, a number of U-boat commanders will take it upon themselves to violate orders prohibiting the carrying of civilians on German ships of war and use their U-boats to rescue citizens, especially women and children, from East Prussia and bring them to the West. In March of 1945, Erich Harms will make such a voyage in U-3023, saving dozens of noncombatants from a life under Soviet occupation.

Dieter Hengen, first watch officer on U-255. COURTESY OF DEUTSCHES U-BOOT MUSEUM CUXHAVEN.

After years of combat, after learning from German military intelligence that he had sunk the *Leopold* with most of her men, Harms at last will have a chance for redemption. But perhaps it will not be enough to put his soul at rest. He will try to settle down with his family to help rebuild Bremerhaven and Bremen after the war and father his fifth daughter Inga. Then he will escape to the sea as a deep ocean fishing captain and put the first West German factory trawler into commission.

His fellow U-boat officers and men will forever be reticent to talk about Harms's life following the war. He will never talk about the war to his family and friends except to make a few oblique comments over the years to his wife Marie about his mentor Reinhart Reche. He will die of a heart attack during a "booze cruise" in 1979, at the age of sixty-nine, in Bremen, and remain a mystery to historians, one of the living casualties of the U-boat war and the Battle of the Atlantic.

Admiral Dönitz and Erich Harms of U-255 at the
award ceremony for the sinking of USS *Leopold*.
COURTESY OF DEUTSCHES U-BOOT MUSEUM CUXHAVEN.

Once in Ireland with CU-16 successfully shepherded to Londonderry
to begin supplying the front-line soldiers, sailors, and airmen as they
prepared for D-Day, the *Joyce* will see the survivors ashore then prepare
for her return convoy run to the United States. Back safely in New
York, Wilcox, Ayres, Ham, Bender, and Kimball will testify before a
naval board of inquiry into the loss of the *Leopold*. They will acquit
themselves well, winning the approval and admiration of the review
board for their grace under pressure and their prescient decisions
during the battle and rescue.

During USS *Joyce*'s next eastbound convoy with Task Group 21.5,
she will encounter a strange turn of events that will forever change the
trajectory of some men's lives, including Bob Wilcox's. While escorting
convoy CU-21 to Ireland, the *Joyce* will go into attack mode again after
the tanker SS *Pan Pennsylvania* takes a torpedo seventy miles south of
Nantucket Island. *Joyce* will rescue dozens of seamen from the *Pan Penn*.
Then the *Joyce*, with the help of DEs USS *Gandy* and USS *Peterson*, will
get its prey, driving U-550 to the surface with a depth charge attack.

The U-boat will come up trying to surrender, but the DEs will have
no such thing. They will circle the U-550 for more than fifteen minutes
peppering it with cannon fire from all the weaponry that they can bring

Sinking of German U-550. German sailors arrested in Londonderry by British Marines (lower right). COURTESY NATIONAL ARCHIVES.

to bear. The *Gandy*, the US Navy replacement for the Coast Guard's *Leopold*, will ram the U-boat as well. Meanwhile, the shooting from the circling destroyer escorts will set up a dangerous cross-fire situation in which men on the *Peterson* will be wounded by friendly fire and the torpedoed *Pan Penn*, wallowing a mile away, will go up in flames when wild firing and stray tracers from the DEs hit gasoline spilling from the tanker.

The crews of the DEs will claim that their vicious attack on the disabled U-boat was in reprisal for the sinking of the *Leopold*. As it was aboard the *Leopold* on the night she attacked U-255, the decks of warships will ring with the shouts of men encouraging each other to kill the bastards. Aboard the *Peterson* the gun crews will continue shooting for minutes after ordered to cease their fire by their officers.

Bob Wilcox will finally get his sister ships to stop firing, and over forty young men will pour out of the U-boat onto the foredeck. The *USS*

USS *Joyce* attacking U-550. COURTESY NATIONAL ARCHIVES.

U-550 sinking after attack by USS *Joyce*, *Peterson*, and *Gandy*.
COURTESY NATIONAL ARCHIVES.

Captain's quarters on the USS *Slater* (same as on the *Leopold*). COURTESY DESTROYER ESCORT HISTORICAL MUSEUM, ALBANY, NEW YORK.

Peterson will move close to the port side of the slowly sinking submarine and stop. At this point the U-boat's first officer will tell his men that they have surrendered and should get into the 44-degree water and swim to the *Peterson* for rescue. But when the Germans swim near the DE, the *Peterson* will pull away, leaving the men to suffer the same fate as 171 men from the *Leopold*.

The crew of the *Peterson* will say they were following orders from their task group commander on the USS *Poole* to return to protect the convoy. They will also say they feared stopping because they might become a target for a second U-boat. Many decades later veteran American officers from the Battle of the Atlantic, speaking anonymously, will admit they felt no obligation to pick up shipwrecked enemy combatants. If the U-boats of Admiral Dönitz could have their Laconia Order, so could American ships known as "hunter-killers."

Burial of a German sailor from U-550 on USS *Joyce* steaming to Londonderry.
COURTESY NATIONAL ARCHIVES.

Despite such harsh sentiments in some circles and the command to neutralize the U-boat and return to the convoy, Wilcox will exceed his orders, and he will stop his ship to rescue thirteen men (including the captain) who have climbed into the tower of the sinking submarine. A photographer on the *Joyce* will take an iconic picture of those submariners pleading for help from their sinking U-boat. Eventually the photo will be on the cover of *Time* magazine, illustrating that the end is coming for the once deadly and feared Ubootwaffe.

Recording the chatter over the TBS aboard USS *Peterson*, seaman Collingwood Harris will hear Wilcox tell the *Gandy* and the *Peterson* in plain English, "I am going in to pick up survivors. If this son of a bitch torpedoes me, I want you to kill every goddamned one of them." What a telling thing for Wilcox to say. It brings his character into sharp focus with its blend of nobility, fear, a sense of fairness, and a heavy dose of bravura.

German survivors of U-550 on USS *Joyce* steaming to Londonderry.
COURTESY NATIONAL ARCHIVES.

During the convoy crossing to Ireland, Wilcox will share his quarters with the rescued officers off the U-boat. Wilcox and his prisoners will have long, daily conversations in his cabin and the wardroom while sharing coffee, pipes of tobacco, and cigars. Following the war, he will correspond with U-550's skipper Klaus Hänert and engineer Hugo Renzmann while they are POWs in England. After their release from prison camp, Wilcox will send them care packages to help them try to rebuild their lives in famished, war-torn Germany. These friendships forged in combat and rescue will continue between the former enemies for the rest of their lives. At one point Wilcox and Renzmann will meet for a series of photographs for the *New York Post* of the former enemies meeting again at the New York Port Authority. Renzmann, now a captain in Germany's NATO naval force, the *Bundesmarine*, will be taking command of a former US Navy destroyer being transferred to Germany for use in the surveillance of Soviet submarines.

To the Heroes of the USS JOYCE (DE-317), its sturdy officers and crew.
"We the survivors of the USS LEOPOLD (DE-319), owe you a debt that never could be paid in any way but our lives. You men will never go down in history for this tragic night of March 9, 1944, but you can rest assured that the twenty-eight men named below will never forget what a great deed you performed beyond the call of duty and risking your own lives in the freezing waters of the North Atlantic. We true COAST GUARDSMEN as each and every one of you are wish you more luck than words can express."

From the men of the LEOPOLD.

Letter from *Leopold* survivors thanking *Joyce*. COURTESY USCG.

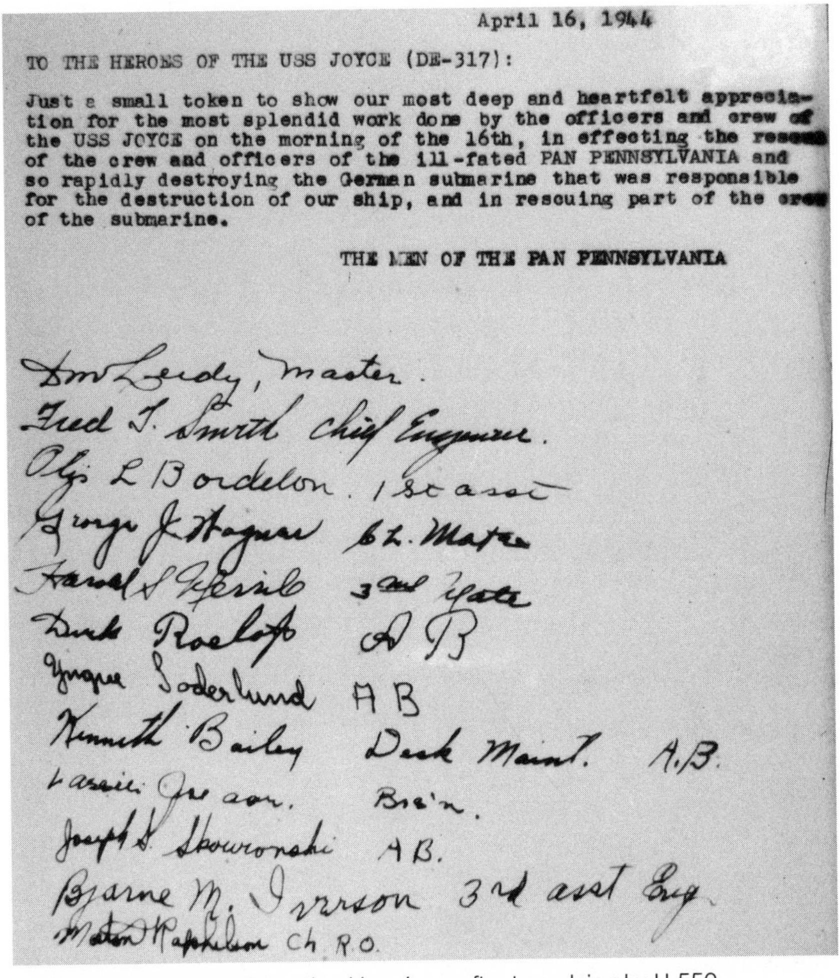

April 16, 1944

TO THE HEROES OF THE USS JOYCE (DE-317):

Just a small token to show our most deep and heartfelt appreciation for the most splendid work done by the officers and crew of the USS JOYCE on the morning of the 16th, in effecting the rescue of the crew and officers of the ill-fated PAN PENNSYLVANIA and so rapidly destroying the German submarine that was responsible for the destruction of our ship, and in rescuing part of the crew of the submarine.

THE MEN OF THE PAN PENNSYLVANIA

[handwritten signatures:]

Don Leidy, master.
Fred J. Smith chief Engineer.
Olp L Bordelon. 1st asst
George J. Wagner 2. Mate
Harold Hersh 3rd Mate
Dirk Roelofs A B
Yngue Soderlund A B
Kenneth Bailey Deck Maint. A.B.
Lassic Jr son. Bos'n.
Joseph H. Skowronski A B.
Bjarne M. Iverson 3rd asst Eng.
Morton Raphelson Ch R.O.

Pan Pennsylvania crew letter thanking *Joyce* after torpedoing by U-550.
COURTESY USCG.

Years after the war, Wilcox will tell his sons that he rescued the Germans because they had surrendered and were no longer a threat. Despite orders from his task group commander to leave the sinking U-boat and its crew and return to the convoy, Wilcox felt it was his duty as a fellow mariner and human being to rescue these men who would surely have frozen to death in the icy seas like their shipmates. It seems clear that in saving the Germans off U-550, Wilcox was in his own way trying to make up for the loss of all those men from the *Leopold* whom he was unable to rescue alive.

Nelson Nersassian, Jr., Survivor of Torpedoing

NELSON NERSASSIAN, JR.

Home on leave awaiting reassignment, Nelson Nersassian, Jr., U. S. C. G., has a thrilling story to tell his parents, Mr. and Mrs. Nersassian, of 4 Dalton parkway, of the torpedoing of his ship in the North Atlantic by an enemy U-boat.

Nersassian, a three-inch gun pointer on a D. E. boat, was on duty when the sub attack began on the evening of March 9. His ship battled one undersea craft, which was kept from striking, but a companion U-boat suddenly launched a torpedo at 8.15 P. M., sending the ship quickly to the bottom. The black gang was hardest hit, as the 18 survivors came principally from the deck crews. In rescuing these men a D. E. boat had to dodge three torpedoes.

Modestly Nersassian admits to saving a seaman who went overside without a life jacket, but before the five hours of their immersion were up he was well nigh exhausted himself, and mighty grateful when an already heavily loaded life raft floated up, submerged waist-deep in the oil-covered waves. Meanwhile, the explosion of depth charges aimed at the destruction of the enemy craft kept up a terrific din. Nersassian is eager for another whack at the enemy.

A native of Salem, where he was born July 5, 1922, the Coast Guardsman is a graduate of Salem High school, class of 1939, and attended Wentworth Institute, Boston, one year in the night division. He was employed at Nelson's spa on Boston street, conducted by his father, before his induction on Jan. 8, 1943. He has two sisters, Rose and Anna, and two brothers, Robert and Arthur, the latter in the U. S. army and recently transferred to the Signal Corps school at Ft. Monmouth, N. J.

The 1944 *Salem News* article on Sparky Nersasian and the sinking of the *Leopold*.

After the war Bob Wilcox will rise to the rank of captain in the US Coast Guard and spend more than thirty years in the service. He and his wife Alice will have a second son and settle in suburban Baltimore. He will survive Alice in retirement and marry twice more. During his retirement in Delray Beach, Florida, Wilcox will spend his time golfing and lending a hand to various charities and service organizations. Although he will serve in many ships, he will always think of the *Joyce* as "my ship," and he will attend DE veteran reunions until his death. At one of these reunions he will have an extraordinary meeting with Erich Harms, who has come as a guest of the veterans. Harms will be there to make peace with his former enemies and to swear that he only fired one torpedo on the night of March 9, 1944. He fired that torpedo out of desperation while under attack by the *Leopold*. He did not fire on the *Joyce*. He will say he would not fire on a rescue ship. Wilcox will believe him . . . but will be forever plagued by the question of who fired those two torpedoes at the *Joyce* that so delayed her rescue of the *Leopold*'s crew.

USS *Joyce* reunion with Commander Robert Wilcox.

Sparky and author Robert, 1944.
COURTESY ROBERT NERSASIAN.

Armand Burgun, survivor of the USS *Leopold*, in 2011.
COURTESY BURGIN FAMILY ARCHIVES.

As for the survivors of the *Leopold* . . . Armand Burgun and six other shipmates will require hospitalization at the British Creevagh Hospital in Londonderry, Ireland, and will take months for their repatriation. The other twenty-one survivors will return to the United States aboard the ships of their escort group, and like the officers of the *Joyce*, each will testify before the board of inquiry into the sinking of their ship. Almost none of these men will return to sea duty. Most will be assigned to the Coast Guard's Manhattan Beach training facility, the place where they began their service, until they can be discharged.

Many of the survivors will get on with their lives. Sparky Nersasian will return to Salem, Massachusetts. It will be five years before he tells his closest sibling Art about what happened to him on the night that the *Leopold* sunk. It will be ten years before he will enter the ocean to swim, and he will never attend crew reunions nor talk about March 9, 1944, with his family and friends. He will live with his aging parents and take over the family convenience store. Nersasian will become a neighborhood personality for fifty years, even entertaining Boston's Bishop Cushing at the store. He will be an inspiration to his siblings, a tender caregiver to his parents, a loving uncle to his nieces and nephews, a golfer, and an expert in the classical music and opera that speaks to his soul. He will never marry. He will continue to make notes about the classical music that he loves in his little brown notebook, and he will die at the age of seventy-five in 1997.

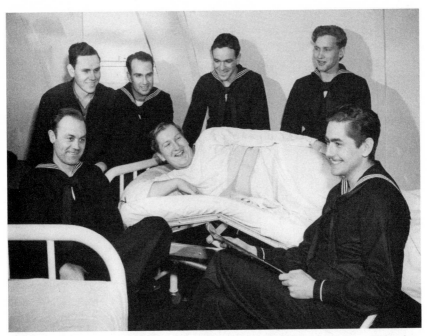

Richard Novotny (*Leopold* survivor) in Creevagh Hospital, Londonderry, Ireland.
COURTESY *USCG HARPOON* MAGAZINE, US COAST GUARD TRAINING STATION, MANHATTAN BEACH, JUNE 1944.

Some of the other survivors like Harry Daube, Richard Novotny, and Gale Fuller will live long and full lives well into the twenty-first century. Fuller will make a life for himself as a power company lineman in his home state of Minnesota. Like Sparky Nersasian he will never marry, but also like Nersasian he will be adored as an uncle. His nephew will remember him as "kind, the salt of the earth, a truly good man."

After recovering from his injuries in Ireland, Armand Burgun will return to the United States aboard SS *Queen Mary*. He will receive his medical discharge from the Coast Guard and finish high school. Then he will attend Columbia University on the GI Bill and become a hospital architect. During the 1960s he will rejoin the Coast Guard as an officer and become the commander of a reserve port security training unit. He will serve for two years on active duty during the Vietnam War until he is declared medically unfit for duty due to the wounds he received the night the *Leopold* sunk. In 2011 he will have an operation on his leg to remove shrapnel from his 1944 wound. Like his fellow survivors, Burgun will rarely speak of his nightmare on the *Leopold*, except to other shipmates at

Tully Square softball team, with Sparky and author Robert in front.
COURTESY ROBERT NERSASIAN.

crew reunions, and never in detail. Like his fellow survivors, he will profess his admiration and debt to Bob Wilcox and the crew of USS *Joyce*.

Other survivors will be less fortunate. After Tory Nersasian starts her online investigation into the story of the *Leopold* in 2010, she will begin to build a network of the *Leopold* survivors' families. Eventually, that network will lead to Bill Miller's daughter Pam. She will unfold the story of a man riddled with PTSD following the loss of the *Leopold*. Her father told her about his guilt related to an incident on the life raft. "Some sailor grabbed him around the neck and pulled him into the water. Half his face was blown off. Both men were trying to hang onto a piece of wood . . . Bill pushed him away and the man went under never to be seen again. Bill felt he killed him."

After the war, Miller joined the merchant marine service on the Great Lakes and became an absentee father. To see him his children will go from their home in Wisconsin to the Blue Water Bridge on Lake Huron to wave at their dad's ship as it passes under. Over the years he will drift back and forth between Wisconsin and Florida. Eventually, he will take a job as a phone company lineman in Florida. One day, while repairing lines, Miller's ladder will be struck by a passing truck. He will die instantly.

The seven men who were hospitalized in Ireland will receive the Purple Heart medal. It is the oldest military decoration in the world still in use, awarded to those wounded or killed as a result of engaging the enemy while serving in the US military. Created by Gen. George Washington, the Purple Heart was the first American award available to the ordinary soldier. Its forerunner, the Badge of Military Merit, dates from 1782 and was a heart cut from purple cloth and edged with lace.

Somehow the twenty-one men who came back with their escort group to New York after the *Leopold*'s sinking will be overlooked and never receive the medal. Seventy years later a Coast Guard official will say that the story of their suffering simply got lost among a legion of over a million American servicemen wounded in World War II.

The world will build two memorials for the lost men of DE 319 at the US Coast Guard Academy. The men will be honored (along with other mariners killed in action) with a memorial at Cambridge American Cemetery in Cambridge, England. The living will get on with their lives. But those who survived will never forget those who didn't, or that

Obelisk at the US Coast Guard Academy memorializing *Leopold* and Escort Division 22. COURTESY ROBERT NERSASIAN.

horrible night of March 9, 1944. In 2012, Armand Burgun will seem to speak for all his fellow survivors when he says, with a solemn note in his voice, "They were just kids, most of them had never been to sea before."

～～～

After about two weeks of testimony and deliberations the naval board of inquiry will draw its final conclusions.

1. That the conduct of the commanding officer, officers, and crew of the *Leopold* during the attack, torpedoing, and while abandoning ship were in accordance with the highest traditions of the Naval service.

2. That the conduct of the commanding officer, officers, and crew of the *Joyce* were in accordance with the highest traditions of the Naval service.

3. That the *Leopold* was carrying out an aggressive attack on an enemy submarine in accordance with existing instructions and doctrine.

4. That the operations of the *Joyce* during the night of 9–10 March, 1944, were in accordance with existing instructions and doctrine.

In addition, the board will take note of factors that might have saved lives. The board will write that "Despite the limited number of escorts left to protect a valuable convoy in a known submarine area, the detail of an additional escort to assist the *Joyce* would have been in the interest of offensive action against a known enemy and would have saved the lives of additional members of the crew of the *Leopold*."

Furthermore, "A greater number of the crew of the *Leopold* would have been rescued had there been sufficient life rafts on board to accommodate them." "Life jacket lights would have been of great value." The board will conclude that "lifebelts of the oral inflation type are not the most efficient or dependable," "rubber life-saving suits would be of great value in protecting men in the water," and "the most effective means of getting survivors aboard the rescue ship is to put men in the water to assist."

Sister Anne (age eighty-nine) receiving Purple Heart for brother Sparky.
COURTESY ROBERT NERSASIAN.

Some of these recommendations will get quick implementation. For example, on her very next voyage the *Joyce* will sail with two additional life rafts. And when the *Joyce's* escort group encounters U-550 torpedoing the *Pan Pennsylvania* off Nantucket in April 1944, the task group commander will assign three, not two, DEs to the hunt for the U-boat and the rescue of tanker crew. But it will take the Coast Guard decades before they employ cold-water survival suits and rescue swimmers.

Sparky and Massachusetts State Representative Michael Ruane.
COURTESY ROBERT NERSASIAN.

Sparky Nersasian's Purple Heart.
COURTESY ROBERT NERSASIAN.

As for getting Purple Hearts for all twenty-eight survivors or finding out who really shot torpedoes at the *Joyce*? It will take almost seventy years and, as a member of Sparky Nersasian's family will say, "Persistence, dedication and just plain, old-fashioned heart."

Purple Hearts for the Boys

As I mentioned in the introduction to this volume, my family's encounter with the violent, sad, and heroic story of the loss of USS *Leopold* started during the summer of 2010 with my adult daughter Tory rediscovering her taped interview with my brother Sparky about the loss of his ship . . . and my own connection to the *Leopold* might have ended on that warm May morning when the Coast Guard awarded Sparky's long-deserved Purple Heart posthumously.

I will never forget that day. At 0900 hours on the bright, warm morning of May 21, 2011, my family gathered around a huge, stone fireplace

Admiral Neptun, Sparky Nersasian with his Purple Heart, the author, and Nersasian's sister Anne, May 21, 2011. COURTESY ROBERT NERSASIAN.

in an event pavilion at the former Coast Guard base at Winter Island in our hometown of Salem, Massachusetts. A convoy of Coast Guard cars and vans rolled up, complete with a color guard in full dress uniforms and a rear admiral with the deeply allusive last name of Neptun.

Rear Adm. Donald A. Neptun stood between the American flag and the Coast Guard flag poised on either side of the fireplace and told our gathering that this was a very special moment because we were all gathered to honor a "veteran who was forgotten, if you will. . . ."

When Neptun said none of this would have happened without the relentless efforts of Dr. Tory Nersasian, I felt a lump rising in my throat. Waves of emotion surged through me. I was proud of Tory for making this chance to honor my brother happen. I was proud of Sparky for his wartime service, for his will to survive . . . for his unwavering love and commitment to his family, his country, and his shipmates.

But there were harder emotions. The old pain of loss. I felt the death of my brother. And here was my sister Anne standing to my left. She was eighty-nine. A sense of the transience of life started to weigh on me. In my mind I could hear the words in an e-mail from Fran Bradley's granddaughter—"I would give anything to have known my father." I felt her pain, felt the pain of all the families who lost men on the *Leopold*.

For a moment it was as if my brother's shipmates were rising from the sea just outside this room. I could tick off the names of the dead—"ANCHALES, Basilio; ANTIOR, Jerome; ASTYK, Vincent Edward. . . ." I could almost hear a chorus of faint voices pleading for a little remembrance, for a little justice, for a little recognition for their sacrifice. Voices pleading for closure for their families. Twenty *Leopold* survivors, including Sparky, had not received their Purple Hearts. The world had all but forgotten them and their ship. Except for those folks gathered at this ceremony, few people knew how the 199 officers and men on the *Leopold* suffered. The history books and Internet were still confused about why they could not be rescued.

From somewhere at the back of my brain or deep in my chest, I heard Sparky's voice asking, "What about all those other guys who didn't receive their Purple Hearts?" What about the families who are still hurting and looking for answers? What about their need for closure and peace?

Then I remembered something that my sister Anne had said a few minutes earlier when a Coast Guard lieutenant asked if she could stand during the presentation to receive the Purple Heart on behalf of the family.

"He was my brother. I could stand all day."

Like our father who escaped the Armenian Holocaust, like Sparky who survived the frigid North Atlantic against all odds, Anne was summoning deep reserves of inner strength. She was teaching me, *personal concerns be damned*. With Tory trying to recover from a brain injury from an auto accident, I had to pick up the cause of the *Leopold's* unrecognized heroes.

———

Sparky's words had haunted my daughter Tory. After listening to his voice on her old tape, she felt like she had become one of those characters in a Kurt Vonnegut novel who has become unstuck in time. Part of her was sitting in the sunny living room of the home in the hills above Atascadero, California. Another part of her was in that icy water, clawing her way aboard that raft, asking Luke Bobbitt to punch her in the face to keep her awake, keep her alive. She began to live with the lost ship and its crew.

While surfing the web in search of more details about the loss of Sparky's ship and 171 of his shipmates, she hit upon the Destroyer Escort Sailors Association (DESA), and its website. On the web page entitled "Seeking Shipmates or Ship Information," she unearthed about thirty posts related to the *Leopold*. They were heart-wrenching.

I am the son of an officer _____ _____ aboard USS Leopold *and have just discovered this site. Anyone with information about my dad please contact me. Thank you. I was a baby and never knew him.*

My father was killed on 9 March 1944 on the USS Leopold. *I was hoping to contact anyone who knew him.*

I am a relative of a man who gave his life saving many others on the USS Leopold. *I am also looking for survivor information.*

Seeking any info . . . especially crew logs, pictures, survivors.

God Bless all who served and gave the ultimate sacrifice for our freedom. You are not forgotten.

There was also some helpful, if not hopeful, news.

Our family has a relatively complete declassified account of what happened in the engagement and we would be willing to share it with other members of the Leopold *family.*

The Coast Guard Academy has a tribute to the men of the Leopold *in the chapel on a small plaque and in the garden behind the chapel is a very nice memorial stone . . . I was their only child losing my dad at 15 mos old. It is nice to visit this site and read of others who may have known my dad.*

A survivor, as posted by me before, has become very ill and is getting worse. He has been to the hospital. And was Lying in ICU not long ago but now its just gotten Worse. He is a great man. Over the last few days I have found out a bit more information that makes more and more sense. 1+1=2 so I did find some answers and that my grandpa was braver than I knew and did so much!

I was born after my brother died so have nothing but other people's memories to "know" him so am grasping at straws to learn as much as I can about his last day of life. So far it has not been a pretty sight. War is so cruel and unforgiving. Any contact would be appreciated.

My Uncle _____ _____ is one of the 28 survivors of the USS Leopold. *I would be able to contact him if you are a survivor as well. He would love to hear from you.*

Overwhelmed with emotion, Tory found herself adding her own messages to the thread, offering to share Sparky's tape with other *Leopold* families. As her research and networking deepened, she brought me fully into her quest to get Sparky his Purple Heart. And as the service inched its way toward a decision about whether to award the Purple Heart to Sparky, we discovered that Harry Daube was not the only living survivor of the *Leopold* tragedy. There was at least one other, Armand Burgun. Injured during the loss of his ship and hospitalized after the rescue, Burgun had received his Purple Heart during the war.

— ∿ —

Our involvement with the *Leopold* families turned more personal when the granddaughter of Charles Francis Bradley, Sparky's gun captain, shared letters from her grandfather, highlighting a love story of a marriage and family cut short by war and his death.

Fran and Dorothy Bradley married in 1937. When the war broke out, Fran was a reservist in the Marines. He left his job as a police officer and volunteered for active duty service with the Coast Guard. He was assigned as a marine guard at a Coast Guard facility on the Great Lakes and took his family with him. Dorothy got pregnant and gave birth to Mary Francis on Christmas Eve, 1942. Then Bradley got transferred.

Writing from the Coast Guard receiving station in Miami, Florida, he worried:

I'll be a total stranger to my own daughter and it is a funny feeling trying to imagine my getting acquainted with my own daughter. I hope you will always lie a little and tell her that her father was a fine man just in case the inevitable happens a little sooner than we expect.

In another letter from Miami Bradley waxed sentimental; he was feeling that his time ashore was running out:

I want so much to gather you both in my arms at least one more time before I shove off. You really know that there is a war on here by all the activity and they are rushing to get us out as fast as they can. There are thousands of men, young, in between, and oldish men, that is for War. . . . It's hard to realize that I will be going into actual combat in the next two or three months. Our complete happiness depends on my coming home with a whole skin. I am not afraid by the thought of what could happen.

As the shipyard in Orange, Texas, rushed the *Leopold* to completion, Bradley sent off another letter:

You'll never know how much I love you both and miss you terribly much. I want to be there on my baby's first birthday so just in case I miss it, just set a place at the table and make believe that I am there.

By December 1943 the *Leopold* was in New York preparing for her convoy trip to Casablanca. Bradley knew that he would not be getting shore leave to run to Dorothy and Mary Francis, who were still in Wisconsin. He looked ahead to Christmases that would never be:

Watta time we will have then. I'll have you, you'll have me and we both will have Mary Francis who will grow up to be a wonderful girl like her mother is.

He posted one last Vmail letter home on February 9 from New York before sailing off to his death. He may already have had a sense that these were the last words that his wife Dorothy and their daughter Mary Francis would ever receive from him. He may already have had a sense that this was a letter from a dead man.

Hello Honey
*   Just a little short letter to let you know that I am still OK and in the pink of health. Would give ten bucks for a quart of that good milk you have and another ten for a gang of your fried chicken. You and M.F. must be real buddies by now . . .*
*   Ever since you mentioned another ring, I have thought a lot about it and so you can figure that you have it coming as soon as I get home. I think also that we need a new car but only after the house is fixed up. Then you can run me to work and pick me up too. And on my*

day off we can have picnics in the park with the dog for Mary Francis,
I think a Springer Spaniel would be just about right.

I've been wondering how our trees are coming along, I hope they
will be large and shady by the time Mary F. grows up. I want her
to have everything we have and then some. If she favors you in your
ways and mannerisms I know she will be a wonderful little lady. And
that is the way it will all turn out. Miss you a lot and just waiting to
hold you both again in my arms.

All my love and devotion,
Fran

—✦—

Every time another *Leopold* family shared its collections of photos and
letters with Tory and me, my heart hurt. Tory's discoveries through the
DESA website and memories of Sparky's Purple Heart ceremony were
keeping me awake at night. Like Tory I had begun to live with the *Leopold* and its men. Then, one day during the summer of 2011, I got a call
from a man named Harry Stillwell. He was frustrated. Like Tory and
me, he had been snared by the story of the *Leopold* and her survivors. His
uncle Gale Fuller was one of those men. He had heard his uncle's story
about being doused in fuel oil and paddling to the *Joyce* on a staging
plank with Jeremy Bowen. And he had discovered that the Coast Guard
gave Harry Daube the Purple Heart in 2010. Since that discovery, Stillwell had been on a quest of his own to get the Purple Heart for his uncle.
He had been totally unaware of Tory's efforts on behalf of Sparky until
just a few hours earlier.

"I've been hitting a brick wall with the Coast Guard," he told me.
"They don't seem to want to talk to me."

Just about the only encouragement that he had gotten from the coasties
was that the Office of Awards and Ceremonies had given him my phone
number along with a suggestion that maybe we would have a productive
talk. Now Stillwell was calling to ask how my family got the Purple Heart
for Sparky. How did we navigate the Coast Guard bureaucracy?

"I really want to get this award for Uncle Gale." Stillwell's voice
sounded tired but resolute. "He deserves it. It would mean the world to
him, and he's not getting any younger."

"Wait a minute." I heard Sparky's voice saying, "Holy shit." "Are you telling me that your Uncle Gale Fuller is still alive? Harry Daube and Armand Burgun are not the last living survivors?"

"That's right."

"Does the Coast Guard know this?"

"That's what I've been trying to tell them, but . . ."

"Alive? He's alive? And he never got the Purple Heart?" The words were coming from *my* mouth, but the voice sounded like Sparky's. It was as if he was right here in the room.

"Uncle Gale's in assisted living."

"I'll do anything and everything I can to help your Uncle Gale," I said. Then on a whim I ask, "Do you think he would be willing to share his story with me?"

⁕

In mid-July of that same summer, a box the size of a case of wine arrived at my front door. The box came from the office of a historian for the US Coast Guard headquarters, and I had been waiting for weeks to get it. I hoped like hell that this box contained the key to unlocking the true story of what really happened to the *Leopold*, the *Joyce*, and all those shipwrecked men on the night of March 9, 1944, I hoped I would find evidence that I could use to help Gale Fuller get his Purple Heart. And maybe if I really got lucky, I would find evidence in this box to explain why the *Joyce* could not start her rescue for three hours. Was she under torpedo fire by U-255? Was there a second German U-boat involved?

Since first hearing from Harry Stillwell, I had been in a bit of a furor to uncover more of the *Leopold*'s story and to get the Purple Heart for Stillwell's Uncle Gale. I had taped a conference call with me, Fuller, Stillwell, Fran Bradley's granddaughter, and assorted other family members of *Leopold* crewmen. Fuller talked about how the boys on the ship called her the Leapin' Leo. He told us the stories of the shakedown cruises to Bermuda and Casablanca. He remembered yelling out to the men on the *Joyce* and paddling to the rescue ship on a plank with Jeremy Bowen. His voice broke when he responded to someone's request for more details about the other men in the crew.

"I'm sorry they didn't all live," he said. "I've spent the last sixty-five years trying to forget."

This man was still hurting. Maybe getting his Purple Heart would bring him a little peace.

⌒〜⌒

One of my favorite places to relax and reflect is a little beach beyond the ruins of Fort Pickering on the former Coast Guard base at Winter Island where Admiral Neptun awarded Sparky's Purple Heart. Since the box of copied documents from the Coast Guard had arrived, I had been coming here almost every day to enjoy the July sun, the sparkling blue water, the sailboats riding the breeze. And, of course, I came with my box of photocopies from the Coast Guard to read.

Amid my box of copies I found a most astonishing document with "CONFIDENTIAL" typed above the heading:

RECORD OF PROCEEDINGS
of a
COURT OF INQUIRY

The eight-day inquiry was convened at the US Navy Yard in New York beginning on March 23, 1944. The subject was the "circumstances connected with the loss of the *USS LEOPOLD (DE-319)*, and the death of and injury to personnel resulting therefrom."

So it was that on this hot summer day, sitting in my aluminum beach chair in the sand at Winter Island in my Bermuda shorts, Army T-shirt, sunglasses, and ball cap, I began reading the transcript of the BOI. As I came to the final pages, I was feeling overwhelmed by all of this information and contradictory testimony from the survivors of the *Leopold* and crewmen on the *Joyce* about whether one or multiple U-boats were involved in the battle. Worse, I was feeling gut-punched by the emotional stories of the Leapin' Leo's survivors testifying in detail about the mass death of their shipmates. The BOI concluded that the excessive loss of life was due to only one rescue ship, the rescue ship's being delayed and hampered by torpedo attacks, the debilitating effects of prolonged exposure to cold air and water, and weakening of morale due to the loss of hope.

On the last page of the findings, my eyes almost popped out of my head as I read the thirty-seventh and final finding of the board.

"The twenty-eight survivors listed in Finding 20 [all the surviving crew] are entitled to the award of the Purple Heart in accordance with General Order 186 and Alnav 20-44."

How could the Coast Guard possibly deny Gale Fuller his Purple Heart now?

Sixty-eight years to the day after the sinking of USS *Leopold*, Seaman 1/C Gale Fuller stood at the podium in the recreation room of Minnetonka Assisted Living Facility. He looked out over a crowd of more than a hundred people that included the mayor of his town of Minnetonka, Minnesota, a cadre of active duty Coast Guard officers and sailors, a host of service veterans wearing unit and ship ball caps, friends, family, and members of the press. Behind him was an easel displaying a picture of the *Leopold* being launched at Orange, Texas, next to photos of Fuller as a young seaman with a gentle smile on his face.

Seaman Gale Lanteen Fuller, survivor of the USS *Leopold*. COURTESY USCG.

Gale Fuller's Purple Heart.
COURTESY USCG.

Now a man of eighty-eight years, he walked with a cane. But he had decided that leaning on it was not an option, so he held it dangling from his left hand. He was no longer as tall as he was in 1944, but he looked strong with the broad back and thick chest of a man who had labored with his body all of his adult life. There was a blue Coast Guard ball cap on his head. A US Coast Guard commander had just saluted him and pinned the Purple Heart medal on his chest next to his striped suspenders. The medal shimmered amid flashing cameras.

He thanked everyone for coming, then he gathered himself, shoulders back, chin up, the way the drill instructors taught him to do at boot camp.

"I really appreciate this. I've never been awarded anything before."

The crowd grew hushed. Just as strong emotions started to swirl among the people in the room and some began to wipe tears from the corners of their eyes, Fuller spoke again.

"I really don't think I deserve this one.... All I did was get cold." Laughter rippled from his audience. The tension broke. The gentle smile of the young seaman in the photographs spread across the old man's face as he stood before the crowd.

Everyone in the room knew that this was a rare moment in their lives. They were witnessing an unsung hero accept, at last, the laurels due him from

US Coast Guardsman Jerome J. Antior on USS *Leopold*, lost at sea.
COURTESY PAMELA ANTIOR FAMILY ARCHIVES.

his government and his country. Gale Fuller had survived the sinking of the *Leopold* by floating on a plank and paddling it to the rescue ship with Jeremiah Bowen and the dying Ens. C. W. Valaer. Then, after his return to the States following the catastrophe, and unlike most of the other survivors, Gale Fuller requested sea duty and served on other Coast Guard ships in both the Atlantic and Pacific Campaigns until 1946.

Every few days following Fuller's award of the Purple Heart, a family member of the *Leopold* crew was making contact with me. Extraordinary stories were surfacing about the men of the *Leopold* and their families. I heard from Linda Chapman, the sister of Walter Ward, lost in the *Leopold* tragedy, and I felt a strange and immediate kinship with this woman. The carpenter's mate who died in Sparky's arms was her older brother, Walter Ward. My skin tingled . . . especially after Chapman told me that her mother had a premonition on March 9, 1944. She sensed that something had happened to her son and that she would never see him again. She knew that USS *Leopold* had sunk.

Admiral Papp with Pam Miller, daughter of *Leopold* survivor Bill Miller, Washington, DC, May 23, 2013. COURTESY ROBERT NERSASIAN.

Peter Cone, officer on USS *Leopold* (portrait).
COURTESY CONE FAMILY ARCHIVES.

A similar story came to me from the second cousin of Pete Cone, the *Leopold*'s executive officer who was lost when the line to him from the *Joyce* broke. Second cousin Berkley Cone wrote me:

On the night of March 9, 1944, Pete's parents Boots and Aunt Sarah Cone were in New Orleans. During the night Sarah had a premonition that Pete was standing on the bow of his ship. In the morning she asked her husband to return to Richmond [Virginia], as she feared for Pete's safety. Within a few days Boots received a telegram that Pete was missing in-action. . . . Amazingly, he did not reveal this news for several days. Maybe he held out hope that Pete would be found alive by some miracle. Finally, as hope faded he approached Sarah at the dinner table. . . . Boots simply informed his beloved wife that Pete was missing-in-action and presumed dead. Sarah's reaction was stoic silence; she did not even excuse herself from the table . . .

It is said that Sarah, on March 9th of each year, sequestered herself in her room to grieve. . . . They had a painting commissioned of Pete in uniform and a little light illuminated it in the guest room of their apartment. The flame was kind of like a flame burning for a lost son, their lost mariner.

Several families mailed and e-mailed me service records of lost loved ones along with painful memories. Jerome J. Antior's family told how his mother used to sit on her porch, waiting for her son to walk up the street, months after he had been reported missing-in-action.

Now thoroughly enthralled with the story of the *Leopold*, I found myself in a conversation with the son and granddaughter of Bob Wilcox, skipper of the *Joyce*. I learned that the captain of the *Joyce* forever worried over who or what fired those torpedoes at his ship on the night of March 9, 1944. During five decades following World War II, Wilcox became determined (if not obsessed) to unravel the mystery and to absolve himself and his crew of any responsibility for the deaths of 171 men from the *Leopold*. He attended a symposium on the convoy battles of the North Atlantic, repeatedly queried US naval intelligence offices, and corresponded with the preeminent German naval historian Dr. Jürgen Rohwer, a history professor at the University of Stuttgart, Germany, and a leading authority on U-boats.

US Coast Guard headquarters in Washington, DC. COURTESY ROBERT NERSASIAN.

None of his inquires turned up a smoking gun. Eventually, Wilcox became convinced that U-255 acted alone and fired just one torpedo on the night of the *Leopold* sinking. He died in 1995 still believing that the *Joyce* had been under fire from two torpedoes on the night of March 9, 1944. He was still chasing after answers with correspondence right up to his death. He was buried at Arlington National Cemetery with full military honors, including a horse-drawn caisson.

⌐⌐⌐

I wondered whether Wilcox was just grasping at straws or whether this observation about the *Leopold's* torpedoes was a slowly emerging apprehension of things seen and yet unseen. But a wave of loss and bewilderment had caught up to me, and I couldn't seriously explore the mystery surrounding the unknown source of those torpedoes. I was on the verge of retreating into my world of semi-retirement and golf when I got a call from Coast Guard headquarters followed by a blast e-mail to Coast Guard authorities saying,

> *Good Afternoon,*
>   *The Vice Commandant approved the award of the Purple Heart on 7 November, 2011 for the USS* Leopold *Survivors . . .*

For the first time in months, I wanted to stand up and shout, "Hallelujah."

⌐⌐⌐

On May 23, 2013, the commandant of the US Coast Guard, Adm. Robert J. Papp Jr., convened a gathering of veterans and families at Coast Guard headquarters in Washington, DC, to present the Purple Heart to the families of the eighteen sailors from the *Leopold* who had never been honored. I was there with the vets' families, coming from as near as Delaware and as far away as Kansas. The Wilcox family was there, along with Pete Cone's and Bill Miller's.

Admiral Papp presented the Purple Heart to Bill Miller's daughter Pam as a representative of the *Leopold* survivors. Later, in front of a Coast

Commandant of the US Coast Guard Admiral Papp in Washington, DC, at Coast Guard headquarters honoring the USS *Tampa* and *Leopold*, May 23, 2013.
COURTESY ROBERT NERSASIAN.

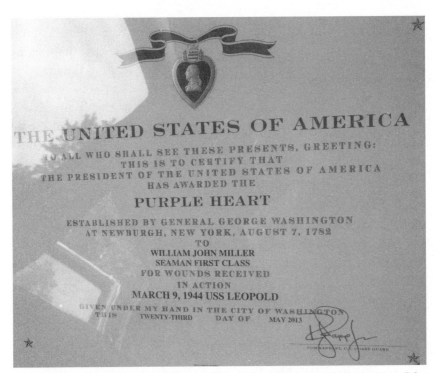

Purple Heart for William John Miller, survivor of the USS *Leopold*, Washington, DC, May 23, 2013. COURTESY ROBERT NERSASIAN.

CITATION TO ACCOMPANY THE AWARD OF

THE PURPLE HEART

TO

SURVIVING CREWMEMBERS

UNITED STATES SHIP LEOPOLD

The Purple Heart is hereby presented in honor of the survivors who received injuries in the sinking of the United States Ship LEOPOLD. At approximately 2000 on 9 March 1944, the LEOPOLD was struck by an acoustic torpedo fired from U-255. Under the command of Lieutenant Commander Kenneth C. Phillips, USCG, the LEOPOLD served as a convoy escort protecting ships carrying critical Allied war material in European waters. At 1950, the LEOPOLD reported a radar contact and sent a message "this looks like the real thing". The convoy began zigzagging and the LEOPOLD was ordered to intercept. After firing two star shells (flares), the crew began firing on the U-boat. The U-boat made an emergency dive, but as she went down, a torpedo was fired and struck the USS LEOPOLD on the port side. One hundred-seventy one people, including 13 officers and 158 enlisted Coast Guardsmen perished that night. Twenty-eight survived their plight and were rescued by the USS JOYCE. The distinguished record of the officers and crew of the LEOPOLD is most heartily commended and is in keeping with the highest traditions of the United States Coast Guard.

Inscription on the Purple Heart for surviving members of the *Leopold* crew, Washington, DC, May 23, 2013. COURTESY ROBERT NERSASIAN.

Guard memorial in Arlington National Cemetery, Papp's remarks grew personal. He said that sometimes it's good to view events not through the lens of time, but through the perspective of those there in the moment. "From that perspective you can better understand those who were there and know something—some measure—of what they were feeling. . . ."

Then he added, "Standing here . . . I feel much more. I also feel a sense of gratitude for the sacrifices that have been made. . . . Not just by those who gave their life in service, but for the husbands and wives and sons and daughters left behind."

Amen, I thought.

US Coast Guard War Memorial, Arlington National Cemetery, Washington, DC, the site of the ceremony honoring the USS *Tampa* and *Leopold*, May 23, 2013.

WELCOME

U.S. COAST GUARD CHIEF PETTY OFFICERS ASSOCIATION
WASHINGTON, DC CHAPTER

DONOR RECOGNITION

RESTORATION OF THE
U.S. COAST GUARD WORLD WAR MEMORIAL
ARLINGTON NATIONAL CEMETERY

WOMEN IN MILITARY SERVICE FOR AMERICA MEMORIAL THEATER

★ ★ ★ ★

MAY 23, 2013

Thank you for joining us as we commemorate this amazing accomplishment
in honor of the generous support of those that made it all possible.

US Coast Guard War Memorial Rededication Program honoring USS *Tampa* and *Leopold*. COURTESY ROBERT NERSASIAN.

JOHN L. BENDER
6233 Walhonding Road
Bethesda, MD 20816

12 June 1995

Dear Shipmates —

Our captain was buried in Arlington National Cemetery on Thursday, 8 June 1995, with full military honors. I don't need to remind you that we are alive today because of the leadership of Robert Wilcox. He was a fine seaman and a brilliant tactician, and a truly nice guy as well.

The weather on 8 June was good, with scattered clouds, breezy, warm and humid. The service commenced in the Old Chapel, with Bob's son Richard leading. From there, a long slow cortege wound down to the grave. As always, the military pomp and ceremony were impressive. At the head of the procession was a small marching band, followed by colors and the color guard, the caisson drawn by six horses with

Lieutenant John L. Bender of USS *Joyce*'s letter (page 1) to crew, describing Captain Wilcox's burial at Arlington National Cemetery. COURTESY DESTROYER ESCORT HISTORICAL MUSEUM, ALBANY, NEW YORK.

four riders, a lead horse and rider, the flag-draped casket, a dozen honorary pallbearers from HQS (most of them captains), and then the string of cars carrying the mourners. There was a brief ceremony as the coffin was placed in the grave; three precise volleys were fired; taps was played (I've never heard it played so beautifully); the flag was carefully folded and presented to Mrs. Wilcox. The entire ceremony had lasted approximately an hour and a quarter.

I told Mrs. Wilcox that I was there representing Bob's shipmates from USS JOYCE, and she seemed pleased. Our wreath was prominently placed, red and white flowers, and a black ribbon which read simply SHIPMATES USS JOYCE.

John L. Bender.

Lieutenant John L. Bender of USS *Joyce*'s letter (page 2) to crew, describing Captain Wilcox's burial at Arlington National Cemetery. COURTESY DESTROYER ESCORT HISTORICAL MUSEUM, ALBANY, NEW YORK.

The Mystery Unraveled

In my interviews with the surviving veterans of the *Leopold* and the *Joyce*, I discovered that over the decades following the catastrophe, the vets had evolved a theory of what really happened on the night of March 9, 1944. Gale Fuller claimed, "We fell for the oldest trick in the book." He believed that the Kriegsmarine used U-255 as a decoy to lure the *Leopold* and the *Joyce* into the sights of a second submarine that may have fired the deadly torpedo at the *Leopold* and fired twice at the *Joyce*. Most of the men subscribe to some version of this theory. A number of men on the Joyce reported seeing the wakes of the two torpedoes barreling down on their ship. Some *Leopold* survivors claimed they saw the periscope or the tower of a second U-boat.

To get a German perspective on the battle, I enlisted the help of researcher Andreas Schalomon in Frankfurt. He had just helped six deep wreck divers from the United States engage with the veterans and their families of the wreck of U-550 that they had found seventy miles south of Nantucket. As described in this book, the U-boat had been sunk by USS *Joyce* and two of the *Leopold*'s other sister ships, the *Peterson* and the *Gandy*, a month following the *Leopold* disaster. I also obtained a complete, translated account of all U-255's KTBs of its eighth patrol from the webmaster of uboatarchive.net. From the KTBs, I could see that the Germans were meticulous record keepers and that the official records showed that 255 fired only the one T5 torpedo that hit the *Leopold*. But what if someone in Germany was trying to cover up the fact that 255 fired twice more at the *Joyce*? What if 255's skipper Erich Harms violated a long-standing code of honor shared by naval combatants and attacked a rescue ship?

I asked Andy Schalomon to visit the Deutsche U-boot Museum in Cuxhaven. At the museum he found a narrative about the battle with the

Leopold written by 255's first watch officer Dieter Hengen. It reiterated and underscored the same series of events spelled out in the KTBs sent from the U-boat. At the end of the narrative, Hengen wrote a footnote in reference to a publication that claims 255 fired at the *Joyce*, but missed:

> *We ran Torpedo Tube 1 with opened muzzle doors and also we shot just one torpedo that struck in an incredibly short space of time. Why is it said that the "Joyce" has been missed? Moreover, the shot has been fired under water, (blind) and during the crash dive respectively.*

I still had questions. I wanted to talk to a living U-boat sailor who might remember the deadly battle between U-255 and USS *Leopold*. After months of digging, Schalomon found the last living officer of 255. Horst Selle was a watch officer aboard 255 under the command of Harms before becoming a U-boat skipper himself. In a letter, Selle gave me a window into the psyches of the boat's crew.

He wrote:

> *Today, we know that an irresponsible leadership used us as cannon-fodder and brought disaster upon human kind. Jörg Zink, pilot officer during the war, wrote in his book* Sieh nach den Sternen— gib acht auf die Gassen, *"After the war, when I read the letters that I had sent home, I found a sentence that I wrote in 1943: "It is impossible. We must not win this war. It would be a disaster for all human kind."'*

Was this what Erich Harms, too, was thinking as he found himself toe-to-toe with the *Leopold*? Perhaps. He emerged only once from the shadows before his death in 1979. He made a pilgrimage to the United States to attend a reunion of the crews of DEs 317 and 319, to meet Bob Wilcox, and to clear the record of what 255 did on the night of March 9, 1944, once and for all. Like Hengen he categorically denied firing more than one torpedo during the battle. Bob Wilcox shook his former enemy's hand and said he believed that what Harms was telling him was the truth as he knew it. The evidence seemed pretty clear. U-255 did not fire on the *Joyce*. But who or what did? Were the American vets right? Was there a second U-boat involved, as many of the *Leopold* and *Joyce* veterans speculated, or was the *Joyce* dodging phantom torpedoes?

I turned to an American friend of Schalomon and a dedicated aficionado of the history surrounding the Battle of the Atlantic. Analyzing all the KTB radio traffic to the boats in the Preussen wolfpack for days before and after the sinking of the *Leopold*, Harold Moyers was able to plot the movements of all the submarines in the group based on their regular and frequent position reports. He concluded that the nearest boat to 255 on the night of March 9, 1944 was U-986. It was within about thirty miles, but its radio traffic shows that it had no awareness of a nearby convoy, no knowledge that 255 had engaged one of the convoy escorts. The KTBs from U-boat headquarters showed that central command had no idea of the situation either and never sent out news of the convoy to Gruppe Preussen.

Did Moyers's analysis of the KTBs mean that the crew of the *Joyce* was mistaken in their belief that they were fired on by two torpedoes?

—◆—

I was coming to the devastatingly sad conclusion that the *Leopold* had been dodging imaginary torpedoes when something in my mind hiccupped. I remembered reading a 1987 letter from Robert Wilcox to a naval historian with a strange, new insight about who launched those torpedoes at the *Joyce*. "We should not rule out the *Leopold*," he wrote. "Her torpedo tubes were mounted on an undamaged section of her deckhouse. As I recall the reported bearing of the torpedo came close to the reported bearing of her stern section."

Could the former skipper of the *Joyce* have been on to something? The *Leopold* carried three torpedoes that had been armed and ready to fire when she attacked 255. The DE's torpedo launcher lay on the boat deck adjacent to the expansion joint where the ship broke in half. What if those torpedoes got loose and into the water?

In the transcript of the BOI, I found three references to loose torpedoes. Glyone Mahaffy told the board that he saw them lying against the ship's exhaust stack. Richard Forrester saw one loose Mark 15 torpedo resting on the 20mm ready ammo box. Warren Young said, "They were smoking or steaming a little bit."

A further review of the BOI shows the sound officer on the *Joyce* confirming that both times the *Joyce* detected incoming torpedoes, they were coming from virtually the same position as the wreck. The detection of the first torpedo coincided with the approximate moment when the *Leopold* broke in half. The second torpedo came at the time when the fantail of the ship heaved steeply into the air forcing the forward end of the wreck, where the torpedoes lay, into the water.

Here was circumstantial evidence to support Wilcox's desperate theory. But really, could such a thing happen? Could those loose torpedoes take off for the *Joyce* if they slipped into the water?

I talked with a number of naval weapon experts, but no one could give me a definitive answer until I reached the curator of the Keyport Naval Museum in Keyport, Washington. She passed on my questions to her torpedo expert, a retired Navy master chief torpedoman's mate named Wallace "Dusty" Rhodes. I sent him the testimony from the BOI transcript, and he agreed to research the matter.

MK15 torpedo. COURTESY US NAVAL UNDERSEA MUSEUM, KEYPORT, WASHINGTON.

A week later, Rhodes sent me a blockbuster of an e-mail. It concluded that according to the sailors' reports in the BOI, the *Leopold* had two functional torpedoes that would have been armed with all safety mechanisms removed and programmed for launch at U-255 as the German submarine was diving into the sea on the port side of the *Leopold*. He added that the German torpedo hitting midships where the torpedo rack was located offers the only viable answer to the question of who or what fired on the *Joyce*. The two torpedoes detected by the *Joyce* came from the *Leopold*. Conclusion: not German but American torpedoes delayed the *Joyce*'s rescue efforts until most of the *Leopold*'s crew had frozen to death.

Following this conversation, I received an amazingly thorough written analysis from Rhodes, which read in part:

> *The torpedoes detected in the water the evening of 9 March, 1944, could have well been LEOPOLD's. That is simply the only viable explanation. When sighted smoking by the crew member the weapons received a sufficient amount of sea water to prevent overheating or over speed of the engine. Eventually the weapons slipped into the sea. They could have hung up on ship's structure for a short time and then set off at the last course gyro setting preset into the weapons prior to launch. The detections by JOYCE could have been a single torpedo acquired several times or both torpedoes as they ran to fuel exhaustion. There were no explosions as they hit nothing of sufficient size in their path or did so before their warheads were armed.*

In other words, the *Leopold*'s two functional torpedoes were programmed, "hot," and ready to launch at the time the DE broke in half. When the self-propelled torpedoes slipped into the water as the wreck broke up, the engines in the torpedoes were already revving, and the torpedoes took off under their own power in the direction already set into their gyros. That direction was off the portside of the *Leopold* where U-255 was last seen diving beneath the waves. As it happened, when the *Joyce* approached the wreck, the *Joyce* moved into the same area where the U-boat had been. Unknown to Bob Wilcox, he had conned his ship into the line of fire of the *Leopold*'s torpedoes.

At the conclusion to his e-mail, Rhodes signs off as a "shipmate." It was like the old chief was telling me, "Mission accomplished, sir." As an Army officer, I took this as one hell of a compliment coming from a Navy man.

Then I went searching for one last piece of evidence, to see if I could find independent support for Rhodes's analysis. Both John Bender, the officer in charge of the sound hut on the *Joyce* the night that it was dodging torpedoes, and Bob Wilcox told the BOI that those two incoming torpedoes did not have the high whine of the German electric torpedoes like a T5. They said the torpedoes that they heard sounded like a "train in a tunnel."

Searching the web I found a site called Historic Naval Sound and Video and located recordings used to train Navy sonar and hydrophone operators during World War II. On one recording I heard the whine of a German electrically driven torpedo like the T5 that sunk the *Leopold*.

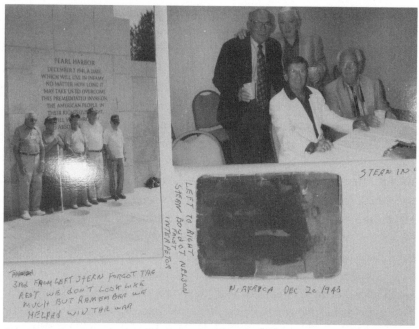

Joyce crewmembers at Pearl Harbor: "We don't look like much but we helped win the war."

I also heard the chugging of an obsolete steam-driven torpedo that the Germans used prior to 1942. Neither sounded like a train in a tunnel. Then I found a recording of an American Mark 14/15 torpedo. I couldn't believe my ears. It sounded like a train in the tunnel. It sounded like death.

Mystery solved. Neither U-255 or any other U-boat attacked the rescue ship. But the *Joyce* was not dodging phantoms. The ship was under attack, not by the Germans but by the *Leopold*'s loose torpedoes. Wilcox and his crew made all the right moves to protect their DE. They had no way of knowing they were trying to avoid friendly fire, no way of knowing that the Germans were no threat to making a quick rescue and saving more lives.

For the better part of his life Bob Wilcox stewed over the source of those torpedoes. I wonder what the skipper of the *Joyce* might say or do in response to the news that he was dodging the *Leopold*'s torpedoes. Quite possibly he would utter a favorite oath of tin can sailors, "Situation normal, all fucked up." Maybe he would cry as he so often did when he remembered that cold night on the North Atlantic and the frosty faces of men like Sparky Nersasian. But I would like to think that Wilcox would reach out for his wife, his children, his grandchildren, his shipmates, and his former enemies. Then he would draw them close. What else can a survivor do?

—Col. Robert Nersasian, 2017

Sources and Acknowledgments

The living survivors of USS *Leopold*—Harry Daube, J. Armand Burgun, and Gale Fuller—welcomed us like family as the idea for this book about their experiences aboard the *Leopold* began to take shape. We were also aided by the living veterans of USS *Joyce*: Gerald Stern, Barney Olsen, Randall Miller, and Monte Coulter. They gave us many hours of their time as we recorded interviews and shared phone conversations with them.

The wives, siblings, children, grandchildren, nieces, and nephews of the veterans of the *Leopold* and the *Joyce* have showed us unlimited generosity in sharing memories with us of their loved ones who, as sailors say of the dead, have "crossed the bar." This book would never have been written if it were not for Dr. Tory Nersasian's devotion to uncovering the story of her Uncle Sparky and his shipmates. And although Sparky has been deceased for more than twenty years, he has left us his daily log of life on the *Leopold* and his taped memories of the attack and sinking on March 9, 1944. We also owe much to the help that we have received from Sparky's siblings Anne, Rose, and Art.

We were able to talk with the family of Bob Wilcox, captain aboard USS *Joyce*. His son Richard and granddaughter Kim Joshi were endlessly helpful in supplying family records that gave us a window into this heroic man. Jeanne Costello, granddaughter of one of the *Leopold*'s lost men Charles Francis Bradley, offered us nineteen letters home from the young sailor. Berkley Cone, nephew of Lt. B. P. Cone, the executive officer on the *Leopold*, shared stories and pictures of his uncle. Linda Chapman and Walter Ward Summers spoke to us about Walter Lee Ward, lost at sea on the *Leopold*. Pam Antior and Mark Bobbitt talked to us about their fathers who served aboard the *Leopold*. So did Charles Webster Valaer Jr.

Pam Miller's father survived the sinking of the *Leopold* only to die tragically years later in an accident. *Sea Classics* magazine has chronicled Lucas Bobbitt's story of survival. Lewis M. Andrews Jr. recorded an invaluable, in-depth interview with Richard Novotny about his survival after the *Leopold* broke in half and sunk.

Many people deserving of recognition have no direct involvement in the sinking. Harry Tangen and his aide Dori of the Escort Sailors Association provided muster lists of contacts and photos of the reunions of *Leopold* and *Joyce* survivors. Author Sylvia Dickey Smith offered us her knowledge of the Orange, Texas, shipyard where all six ships of Task Group 21.5 were built. Her novel *A War of One's Own* (Crickhollow) gives a poignant look into the lives of the shipbuilders. Fred Fairbanks, a seaman on the USS *Kirkpatrick*, told us his humorous stories of Coast Guard service and offered us his knowledge of the *Edsall* Class destroyer escort. Coast Guard historians Bob Browning, Scott Price, and Bill Thiesen shared their knowledge and endless reams of reports, data, and photos. Author Pat Zalewski worked with us in the early stages of research and development.

We have had the help of the six divers who found the wreck of U-550 about seventy miles south of Nantucket Island in 2012—Joe Mazraani, Brad Sheard, Eric Takakjian, Tom Packer, Steve Gatto, and Anthony Tedeschi. We also owe a debt to wreck diver Harold Moyers, who has an absolutely encyclopedic knowledge of U-boats and other ships involved in the Battle of the Atlantic. We can't count the times Harold has shot us e-mail attachments and photos to clarify some question or detail of U-boats or World War II.

The U-550 discovery team shared their decades of research with us, and their libraries. Eric Takakjian presented us with shopping bags full of his personal volumes—with key pages bookmarked—on submarines, destroyers, and merchant ships. Both Takakjian and Joe Mazraani offered us correspondence with researchers, survivors of Task Group 21.5, e-mails from families of dead veterans, and letters of deceased veterans.

During the dive team's research trip to Germany in November 2013, they met with U-550 survivor Albert Nitsche and heard his reminiscences of serving in the Ubootwaffe as gunner and steward. The conversations with Nitsche would not have been possible had it not been for the assistance of our capable and gregarious translators Lisa Svec and Martin Abel in the United States and Andreas Schalomon in Germany.

Schalomon has been an indefatigable researcher in Germany on behalf of this book. He has been instrumental in unearthing critical data and photographs at the Deutsches U-Boot Museum and in helping us to find the families of U-255's crew. The late Horst Bredow's Deutsches U-Boot Museum is a must visit for anyone interested in researching U-boats and the Battle of the Atlantic. Through Schalomon we were able to talk to Erika Harms Hauffe and her sisters, who provided us with a humanizing portrait of their father Erich Harms, skipper of U-255.

Joe Mazraani's correspondence with other survivors' families like that of John Bender, ASW officer on the *Joyce*, also helped us understand the men involved in the battles involving both U-255 and U-550. Despite ill-health Hugo Renzmann, the former engineer aboard U-550, met with the divers during a research trip to Germany. That meeting would have been impossible without the collaboration and help of NDR TV reporter Andreas Schmidt.

We found interviews with Bob Wilcox and other crewmen from the *Joyce* on Vimeo. "Eye Witnesses of World War II, USS Leopold" is a moving posting by diver Mark Munro and filmmaker Rob Sibley. The video gives first-person accounts of the loss of the *Leopold* and a look at brave men who are no longer with us. "Eye Witnesses of World War II, U-550," is another relevant posting by this research team. "Eye Witnesses of World War II, *USS Leopold*," Collingwood Harris's amazing interview about his Coast Guard career, including his service with Escort Group 22, is on the website of the US Coast Guard Oral History Program. Of course, the deck logs and action reports from USS *Joyce* clarified the timetable of the battle and the action from each of the crew's perspective. The post-sinking Record of Proceedings from the board of inquiry investigating the loss of the *Leopold* is a trove of first-person accounts by twenty-one of the DE 319's survivors as well as the officers of the *Joyce* and the escort group commander on the *Poole*.

When it came to following the paper trail surrounding the ships involved in the battle of March 9, 1944, wreck divers Eric Takakjian,

Brad Sheard, and Joe Mazraani offered us action reports, radio messages, depositions, and interrogation reports gleaned through the Freedom of Information Act from correspondence with, and visits to, the Naval Historical Center and the National Archives.

Lisa Svec's German 600 class at Phillips Academy in Andover, Massachusetts, proved enthusiastic, able, and invaluable translators of German war records as well as letters in German written by members of U-boat crews.

Ms. Deneen Day, at the US Coast Guard office of Awards and Ceremonies, Rear Adm. Donald Neptun, the commandant of the First Coast Guard District, and former commandant of the US Coast Guard Robert J. Papp Jr. have been helpful in both our research for this book and in taking the lead to get Purple Heart medals awarded to the entire crew of the *Leopold*. In addition, Rear Admiral Neptun volunteered to write a piece for the front of this book on the US Coast Guard at war.

The Anxiety and Depression Association of America (ADAA), and the PBS show *Perilous Fight* offered us expert insights and statistics about post-traumatic stress disorder (PTSD). For a historical perspective three books on World War II in the Atlantic were invaluable: Samuel Eliot Morison's *The Battle of the Atlantic* (Little, Brown & Co.), Clay Blair's monumental two-volume set *Hitler's U-boat War* (Random House), and legendary diver Gary Gentile's *Track of the Gray Wolf* (Avon Books). Eberhard Rössler's *The U-boat* (Cassell & Co.) has excellent photos and historical documentation of U-boat development. Likewise, there is great historical material on Type IX U-boats in Fritz Kohl and Axel Niestlé's *Vom Orignal zum Modell: UboottypIX C*. Niestlé's book *German U-boat Losses During World War II: Details of Destruction* also adds to the picture. While researching online one day, we came across the website of the Historic Naval Ships Association, hnsa.org. Here was an English translation of the Kriegsmarine's *The Submarine Commander's Handbook*, circa 1943. What insight it gives into the German navy's expectations for Erich Harms as the commander of the U-255. U-boat commander Herbert A. Werner took us into his life on a World War II German submarine through his memoir *Iron Coffins* (Da Capo Press) as did Michael Gannon's *Operation Drumbeat* (Naval Institute Press). Lothar-Günther

Buchheim is not only the author of the novel *Das Boot*, but also the creator of an amazing volume of photos and narrative called *U-boat War* (Bonanza Books), which documents a patrol on a combat U-boat in 1942 with astonishing photos.

The website uboatarchive.net is a trove of information on battles, submarines, ships, and, especially for our research, crew information. Its webmaster Capt. Jerry Mason, USN (ret), came to our rescue with complete translations of the KTBs (radio reports to headquarters) from U-255 during her entire eighth patrol during which she sunk the *Leopold*. Other helpful websites include uboat.net, uboataces.com, sharkhunters. com, and historisches-marinearchiv.de. Nothing is better at illustrating the strain of life aboard a U-boat than Wolfgang Petersen's film version of Lothar-Günther Buchheim's *Das Boot*.

Curator Steve Rosengard at the Museum of Science and Industry in Chicago and former curator Keith Gill shared their vast amounts of research on U-boats with us. The captured German U-boat U-505 is on display in Chicago. The 505 is a national landmark and a keystone exhibit at the museum. It is also only one of two type IXC U-boats to be pre-served for history and a near clone of U-550, which USS *Joyce* battled a month after the sinking of the *Leopold*. The only type VII attack U-boat like 255 in existence is U-995. It is on display at the Laboe Naval Memo-rial on Kiel harbor in Germany and touring her is a step back in time to a frightening yet heroic era for people of all nations.

In researching destroyer escorts, we relied on Lewis M. Andrews Jr.'s *Tempest, Fire and Foe: Destroyer Escorts in World War II and the Men Who Manned Them* (Narwhal Press), *Escort* (W. Kimber) by Denys Arthur Rayner, *The Cruel Sea* (Burford Books) by Nicholas Monsarrat, and the website of the Destroyer Escort Sailors Association, desausa.org. The 1957 film *The Enemy Below* does for DEs what *Das Boot* does for life aboard U-boats. Former destroyer skipper Capt. Ron Trossbach and retired naval officer Dale Hurley helped us to understand the duties of a destroyer captain and his officers during combat. *A Careless Word . . . A Needless Sinking* (American Merchant Museum) by Arthur R. Moore is an excellent resource for researchers looking to find the histories of

American merchant ships sailing in World War II. Additional helpful volumes include John Keegan's *The Second World War* (Penguin Books), Nathan Miller's *War at Sea: A Naval History of World War II* (Scribner), and John Terraine's *Business in Great Waters: The U-Boat Wars, 1916–1945* (Leo Cooper). Another good source is the website usmm.org. Tim Rizzuto, ship superintendent at the USS *Slater* Historical Museum, and the museum's website ussslater.org have been highly elucidating about life aboard destroyer escorts and the ships' weapons and ASW detection equipment.

Mary Ryan, curator of the Keyport Naval Museum in Keyport, Washington, advised us on the workings of the *Leopold*'s torpedoes. So did Dr. Theresa Baus (Head, Technology Partnerships Office Naval Undersea Warfare Center Newport, Rhode Island) and her torpedo expert, Hector Lopez, plus their public relations officer John Woodhouse. Capt. John Markowitz, USN, of Washington, DC, Navy Yard and his father, a retired naval officer, contributed their insights. USS *Kirkpatrick* veteran Fred Fairbanks also weighed in with his own insights and stories about the Battle of the Atlantic.

The man who truly gave us the expert insight to unlock the mystery surrounding the two torpedoes that the *Joyce* claimed to have dodged was torpedoman's mate master chief Wallace "Dusty" Rhodes, who specialized in surface-launched torpedoes. He served in the US Navy from March 1964 until July 1986. After retirement he worked as a government contractor for Vitro Corp and BAE Systems, spending six years at the Naval Undersea Warfare Center, Keyport, Washington.

We found recordings of World War II–era German and American torpedoes in flight at Historic Naval Sound and Video, www.maritime .org/sound. The website for the Naval Historical Center, history.navy. mil, is an excellent site for all things related to US Navy history. The web postings of Capt. John L. Beebe, USNR, Lt. Col. Ted A. Morris on jacksjoint.com, and Collingwood Harris have given us a window into Coast Guard Basic Training at the Sheepshead Bay Training Station at Manhattan Beach, New York.

Finally, this book would never have reached publication without the counsel and energy of our literary agent, Doug Grad, who believed with heart and soul in our story and the concept of the manuscript. Like Doug, our editor at Lyons Press, Eugene Brissie, brought enthusiasm and editorial guidance to our project. Copy editor Joshua Rosenberg and production editor Meredith Dias added insight and sparkle to the text. Layout artist Rhonda Baker worked her magic on the illustrations we supplied and gave a handsome look to this volume.

INDEX

Note: Abbreviation DE stands for destroyer escort. USS *Leopold* survivors are identified by name and the term (survivor). Non-surviving *Leopold* crew members are identified by name only. Officers and crew members of the USS *Joyce* and the submarine U-255 are identified as (USS *Joyce*) and (U-255), respectively.

About the Authors

Randall Peffer is the author of nine nonfiction books, most with a nautical angle, as well as nine crime/suspense novels. His first book, *Watermen* is a documentary of the lives of the Chesapeake's fishermen. It won the *Baltimore Sun's* Critic's Choice Award and was Maryland Book of the Year. His most recent book, *Where Divers Dare: The Search for the Last U-boat* was published in April 2016.

The son of a career naval officer, Peffer holds a 100-ton masters license and has logged over 100,000 miles at sea, mostly in traditional working vessels. He has been the captain of the 55' wooden research schooner *Sarah Abbot* for twenty-nine years. After thirty-seven years teaching writing and literature at Phillips Academy, Andover, he has retired to focus full-time on his writing. He sails out of his home ports of Marion, Massachusetts, and Great Guana Cay, Abaco.

Col. Robert Nersasian is a practicing oral and maxillofacial surgeon. He is a retired associate professor of oral and maxillofacial surgery at Tufts University. Nersasian is also a retired US Army Colonel, having served on active duty during the Vietnam and Desert Storm conflicts. He has published multiple papers in medical journals. Most notably, he is the baby brother of seaman Sparky Nersasian, having been one year old at the time of the sinking of the *Leopold*. He joined his daughter Tory in her quest to achieve recognition of the *Leopold*'s story with the awarding of the Purple Heart to the crew in Washington, DC, presented by US Coast Guard Commandant Admiral Robert J. Papp Jr. on May 23, 2013.